THE BAFFLED PARENT'S GUIDE TO

COACHING 6-AND-UNDER SOCCER

"I highly recommend this terrific book to coaches who want to instill good sportsmanship and the love of the game in their young players while building a solid foundation in basic soccer skills and teamwork."

—Jeremy Gunn, Head Men's Soccer Coach, Fort Lewis College

Look for these other Baffled Parent's Guides

Coaching Youth Baseball
by Bill Thurston

Great Baseball Drills
by Jim Garland

Coaching Youth Basketball
by David G. Faucher

Great Basketball Drills
by Jim Garland

Coaching Youth Football
by Paul Pasqualoni with Jim McLaughlin

Teaching Kids Golf
by Detty Moore

Coaching Youth Hockey
by Bruce Driver with Clare Wharton

Coaching Boys' Lacrosse
by Greg Murrell and Jim Garland

Coaching Girls' Lacrosse
by Janine Tucker and Maryalice Yakutchik

Coaching Girls' Soccer
by Drayson Hounsome

Coaching Youth Soccer
by Bobby Clark

Great Soccer Drills
by Tom Fleck and Ron Quinn

Coaching Youth Softball
by Jacquie Joseph

Coaching Tee Ball
by Bing Broido

THE BAFFLED PARENT'S GUIDE TO COACHING 6-AND-UNDER SOCCER

Introducing Young Players to the World's Most Popular Sport

Includes Time-Tested Games and Fun-Filled Drills

David Williams
and Scott Graham

Camden, Maine • New York • Chicago • San Francisco
Lisbon • London • Madrid • Mexico City • Milan
New Delhi • San Juan • Seoul • Singapore • Sydney • Toronto

The McGraw-Hill Companies

12 13 14 15 16 17 QVS/QVS 19 18 17 16 15

Library of Congress Cataloging-in-Publication Data
Williams, David.
The baffled parent's guide to coaching six-and-under soccer : David Williams and Scott Graham.
p. cm.—(Baffled parent's guides)
Includes bibliographical references and index.
ISBN 0-07-145628-7
1. Soccer for children—Coaching. 2. Soccer for children—Training. I. Graham, Scott. II. Title. III. Series.
GV943.8.W55 2006 2005008434

Questions regarding the content of this book should be addressed to
McGraw-Hill/Ragged Mountain Press
P.O. Box 220
Camden, ME 04843
www.raggedmountainpress.com

Questions regarding the ordering of this book should be addressed to
The McGraw-Hill Companies
Customer Service Department
P.O. Box 547
Blacklick, OH 43004
Retail customers: 1-800-262-4729
Bookstores: 1-800-722-4726

Photographs by Jerry McBride.
Line art characters by Jim Sollers.

Contents

Introduction

So you've signed up—or been enlisted—to coach an age-6-and-under soccer team, and you don't know where to begin.

First, rest assured you're not alone.

The youth soccer boom in the United States has been going on for some time. A smaller, less obvious boom within that boom has been taking place more recently: the huge increase in soccer teams and leagues for very young players.

Increasingly, parents are acting on the fact that though it takes children a while to develop the skills and physical size necessary to play sports like baseball, basketball, and football, their kids can kick a ball around a field with their feet when they're as young as 3. Not content to let their kids do such ball kicking in haphazard fashion, parents are plugging their kids into little-kid soccer leagues in steadily increasing numbers.

By one estimate, about 20 percent of the estimated 13 million children playing organized soccer in the United States today are under age 7. That translates into nearly 3 million preschoolers, kindergartners, and first-graders playing organized soccer—and tens of thousands of parents, grandparents, aunts, uncles, and interested volunteers just like you joining the ranks of little-kid soccer coaches every year.

I was tagged to coach my son's kindergarten soccer team a few years ago even though I'd never played the sport. Fortunately I was teamed to coach with David Williams, this book's coauthor. Unlike me, David's entire life to that point had revolved around the world's most popular sport. In addition, David was a devoted at-home dad. That combination made him a terrific little-kid soccer coach.

Together David and I developed a distinct coaching philosophy and specific teaching techniques for our young players. The results were gratifying. Our kids improved as soccer players, yes. But most of all they learned to love playing the game of soccer.

In the years since, David and I have further researched and refined our 6-and-under coaching methods. In the pages that follow, we present the philosophy, techniques, coaching tips, and practice sessions that have worked best with our 6-and-under players and those of many other coaches. Every word and diagram in this easy-to-read, ready-to-use book is aimed at quickly enabling you to become a great coach to your young players—and to have fun right along with them while doing so.

Scott Graham
Durango, Colorado

About This Book

We've written *Coaching 6-and-Under Soccer: The Baffled Parent's Guide* primarily for beginning soccer coaches. If, however, you're an experienced coach, we believe you'll still learn a great deal from this book. That will be particularly true if your previous soccer coaching experience has been with older players.

Recently we attended the first practice of a group of 4-year-olds with a friendly, easygoing dad as their coach.

"I'm really overqualified for this," the dad told us. "I coached 14-year-olds for the last five years."

The father meant no disrespect to his young players. But it's important to note that his years of coaching older players didn't necessarily prepare him to introduce the sport of soccer to young players. Just as lecture-and-test teaching techniques used by middle and high school teachers obviously don't work with preschoolers and kindergartners, so too the demonstrate-and-drill teaching techniques used to coach older players would be—and in many cases today continue to be—a colossal failure with young players.

The very real fact is that young soccer players are different than older players and so must be coached differently. Those differences are the topic of Chapter 1, Coaching Young Players Is Different.

Chapter 2, Fun-Focused Practices and Games, takes a close look at the thinking behind the techniques laid out in the remainder of this book.

We provide an overview of the game of soccer from the perspective of young players in Chapter 3, The Game of Soccer for Young Players. We also take a quick look at the official rules of soccer your young players will be expected to understand and follow this season.

Chapter 4, Off the Field, walks you through the things you'll need to take care of before your team's first practice to ensure your players have a fun and thus successful season, including the critical job of managing parent expectations.

In Chapter 5, On the Field, we describe the equipment you and your players will need, and we discuss how best to make use of that equipment during practices and games. We also discuss why the right attitude is far and away the most important piece of "equipment" you should bring to each practice with your young players.

We provide solutions and suggestions for dealing with the various behavior-related issues you may face with your young players in Chapter 6, Behavioral Challenges of Young Players.

Chapter 7, Game Day, takes you through the fun and excitement of your young players' games—and why it's so critical for you to de-emphasize winning and losing with your team. In addition, your game-day coaching responsibilities are covered in detail.

In Chapter 8, Basic Ball-Control Skills and the Red Light/Green Light

Drill, we detail skills that will help your young players learn the basics of the game of soccer, and we discuss how to teach those skills to your players by using the simple, fun Red Light/Green Light drill.

At the same time you're introducing basic ball-control skills to your players over the course of your first six practices, you'll reinforce those skills—and have your players repeat them many times over—by running your players through the additional eleven fun drills detailed in Chapter 9, Eleven More Drills and Four More Skills. Numerous tips and hints, as well as suggested story lines, will make it easy for you to run these fun activities—more games than drills, really—with your players.

In addition, we present four additional skills in Chapter 9 for you to begin introducing to your young players as they become ready to learn them.

Chapter 10, Your First Six Practices, includes two sets of specific, minute-by-minute practice sessions. Each practice session includes the introduction of one basic ball-control skill. The skills are introduced in order so that they build on one another. The sets of practice sessions are divided by age—one set of practices for coaching 4- and 5-year-olds, and a second set of practices offering slightly more advanced techniques and drills for coaching a team of 5- and 6-year-olds.

The practice sessions are designed and presented to be easy for you to use. Just photocopy each practice session, stick the copy in your pocket or on a clipboard, and head out the door—everything you need to run each practice will be right there for you.

The Skills Troubleshooting Chart that follows Chapter 10 offers a quick way for you to spot and address any difficulties your young players may have with the ten ball-control skills covered in Chapters 8 and 9.

The Resources section offers a selection of websites and books you may wish to refer to for more information after reading this book.

Once your players have mastered the drills introduced in this book, you and they will be ready for the competition-oriented coaching philosophy and the drills for older players presented in Bobby Clark's *Coaching Youth Soccer: The Baffled Parent's Guide*. Your players also will be ready at that point to try out some of the 125 dynamic, creative games detailed in *Great Soccer Drills: The Baffled Parent's Guide*, by Tom Fleck and Ron Quinn.

CHAPTER 1

Coaching Young Players Is Different

Quick Coaching Guide

Your job as coach is to run fun practices that enable your players to touch and move the ball with their feet as much as possible.

Your job is to serve your players, not your players' parents.

You need focus only on teaching your players the basics of soccer, not advanced aspects of the game.

Children learn by doing, by actively participating in the world around them.

For young soccer players, fun = learning.

When we became first-time soccer coaches of our two 5-year-old children and their teammates, the first thing we did—or, we should say, the first mistake we made—was to turn to one of the many youth soccer coaching books on the market for drills to try with our young players.

At our first practice, we tried a defense-teaching drill, as suggested in the book, that involved kicking balls away from our players as they dribbled—that is, as they kicked their balls around in front of them. When we ran the drill, some of the children whose balls we kicked away collapsed to the ground in tears.

At the end of the second drill we tried—a ball-dribbling relay race also recommended in the book—the last-place team of 5-year-olds was crestfallen.

We quickly learned that young children aren't ready for the competitive aspects of game play that captivate older children and adults alike. We met with success only when we adjusted our coaching strategies accordingly.

The dribbling relay race became a giggle-filled follow-the-leader drill—around bushes, beneath low-hanging tree branches, through ditches, in and out of goals, and between groups of waiting parents. The drill based on kicking away kids' balls became Switch, wherein our young players dribbled a ball until we yelled "Switch!" at which point they had to dart to someone else's ball and dribble it. In each of these drills and others we adapted from books for coaching older players, there were no winners or losers, just lots of fun to be had kicking soccer balls around a grassy field.

Toward the end of our first practice, we attempted to teach our young players the correct way to dribble a soccer ball by seating them before us and demonstrating various ball-control techniques with our feet.

Bad idea.

In an instant our young players were wrestling with one another, shoving their soccer balls up their shirts and pretending they were Santa Claus, picking wads of grass and shoving them down one another's shorts—anything but listening to us.

We looked at each other and sighed. Then we got our players up and playing another game of Switch. As they played, we wandered from player to player, suggesting ways to dribble the ball that conformed with what we'd tried to demonstrate while they were seated. When players actually did what we suggested, we praised them loudly enough for the rest of the team to hear. In search of some of that praise for themselves, other players tried out the suggestions as well. Soon enough our players were dribbling while using basic soccer technique. Best of all, they'd learned that technique while playing soccer.

Steep Learning Curve

Our learning curve as new coaches remained steep. In short order we learned how important it was to our sanity to remember that, like most youth soccer practices, ours were held at the end of the day when our young players were tired and their short attention spans even shorter than usual. In response, we developed vigorous practices that kept our players moving and didn't last too long.

We also quickly came to see that the more our players touched and moved the soccer ball with their feet in practice, the faster they developed as soccer players. In answer to that realization, we turned increasingly to games like Switch and Red Light/Green Light that encouraged all our players to touch and move the ball all the time.

Over the course of our first season, we heard of and adopted the Thousand-Touch Rule for our practices. The rule states that the goal of a good soccer coach should be for the players to touch the ball with their feet at least a thousand times each during every practice. We never actually tried to count the number of times each of our players touched the ball. Rather, the rule reminded us that our primary focus during practices was to play a variety of fun games with our players that, little though they knew it, required them to touch and move the ball with their feet over and over and over again.

By the end of our first season, we'd also learned what every preschool, kindergarten, and first-grade teacher knows: young children thrive on routine. When we developed a set practice schedule and stuck to it, our young soccer players had even more fun because they knew what to expect—and their soccer skills steadily improved as a result.

We didn't invent the successful techniques we present in this book. Instead, because a book for coaching young soccer players didn't exist, we borrowed ideas and adapted techniques for our young players from the many older-kid soccer coaching books on the market. We also compared notes and shared ideas with lots of other coaches of young soccer players.

Over time, we developed practice and game-day routines that carried us through the first two to three years of our children's soccer careers. Only at that point were our kids ready to take on the competition-oriented practice and game-day techniques presented in the dozens of youth soccer coaching books on the market today (including the two best, and best-sellers, of the bunch, *Coaching Youth Soccer: A Baffled Parent's Guide* and *Great Soccer Drills: A Baffled Parent's Guide*).

Your Critical Role

If you're not nervous about taking on the role of 6-and-under soccer coach, here's reason to be: the upcoming season will be the first time most, if not all, of your young players will play an organized team sport. You, as coach, will be your players' introduction to the world of athletics. Do a good job, and your players will finish the season loving soccer and loving their initial exposure to teamwork and team play. Do a bad job, and . . .

Well, there's no need to consider that scenario. Why? Because you really have nothing to be nervous about. Coaching soccer to youngsters is, in fact, easy—as long as you remember two critical points:

- Your young players are *itching to have fun.*
- You're there for *your players, not your players' parents,* some of whom may be more concerned with winning and losing soccer games than with whether their kids are having fun and, by having fun, learn to play and love the game of soccer.

Your job, as a coach of young players, is to run fun practices that enable your players to touch the ball with their feet as much as possible—that is, to *play the game of soccer.* Your job as coach specifically *does not* include teaching your players advanced aspects of the game such as goalkeeping, sideline throw-ins, and position play. Those aspects, often taught by coaches to young players, are aimed at one thing and one thing only: winning young-player soccer games. Coaches who teach such advanced aspects of soccer to 6-and-under players fail to focus on teaching their young players the basic skills they need to learn while they're young so they can build on those skills and win games as older players, when winning and losing actually will matter to them.

In your role as coach to your young players, you'll risk squelching your players' enthusiasm for soccer if you emphasize advanced aspects of the sport and, in so doing, put your desire to win ahead of your job of teaching soccer's basics to your young players through game-like drills that enable you and your players to have loads of fun.

There's a reason many of America's young soccer players come to dread playing on their youth teams as they grow older. As very young players enrolled in soccer programs by their parents, children have no choice but to participate in the types of practices favored by far too many well-meaning but ill-informed coaches that emphasize lap running, line-up-and-wait-your-turn drills, and the teaching of advanced skills—all at the expense of having fun. Eventually, however, players grow old enough to rebel against the years of wind sprints, lectures, and boring drills to which they've been subjected at countless soccer practices over the years. What do they do? They quit the game. Today, 70 percent of all youth soccer players in the United States give up the sport by age 12.

As a coach of 6-and-under players, you can't fix the dropout problem facing youth soccer in the United States today. But by taking note of it, you certainly can start your young players off right.

"In your role as coach to your young players, you'll risk squelching your players' enthusiasm for soccer if you emphasize advanced aspects of the sport and, in so doing, put your desire to win ahead of your job of teaching soccer's basics to your young players through game-like drills that enable you and your players to have loads of fun."

Keeping Fun Foremost

In the early 1900s, the renowned French developmental psychologist Jean Piaget was among the first to recognize that emotion and cognition are constantly intertwined in child development. Put simply, Piaget recognized that children *learn by doing*. He asserted that children cannot and do not learn by merely observing and imitating what they see in the world around them. Rather, as Piaget proved through decades of observational study, children learn by *interpreting* the world around them through their *active participation* in that world.

How, then, to get your young players to actively participate in the practices you hold, and thus learn the game of soccer? By making their participation *fun*.

In his book *Just Let the Kids Play: How to Stop Other Adults from Ruining Your Child's Fun and Success in Youth Sports*, child sports expert Bob Bigelow puts it bluntly: "Kids want to have fun—that is their top priority. Kids want to play."

Not only do young children *want* to have fun, but they *need* to have fun. That's how they learn.

Fun = Learning

As long as you keep that basic theorem in mind, your mission as a coach of young soccer players will remain clearly focused, and your job as a coach will be easy.

The Sport of Choice

Do children first learn how to walk or how to write their names?

Walk, of course, generally around their first birthday. By age 3 children can run and jump . . . and kick a soccer ball. By 4 they can skip and balance on one foot for several seconds . . . and direct the movement of a soccer ball with their feet.

Not until age 5, however, do children begin to develop the hand-eye coordination necessary to write their names . . . and play baseball, basketball, and football. Even then, that coordination is rudimentary at best. Not until age 6 have most children developed the high level of hand-eye coordination necessary to grasp a pencil and write their name legibly . . . and shoot a basket, catch a football, or hit a moving baseball.

No wonder, then, that soccer has become the sport of choice among parents of young children in America today. Those parents recognize that not only is soccer a sport their children are *capable* of playing, but that, when presented correctly, soccer is pure, 100 percent *fun* for little kids to play. As a coach, your job is simply to make that recognition a reality for your eager young players.

Fun-Focused Practices and Games

Quick Coaching Guide

Soccer is all about touching, moving, and passing the ball with the foot and body in fluid and creative ways.

Your players will benefit from practices made up of fun, touch-oriented drills that build one upon another.

Touching the ball with the foot at this young impressionable age is the key to becoming a good soccer player—and thus a player who enjoys the game of soccer.

Introduce soccer to your young players not as the competitive game it is, but as something that is *just plain fun.*

We've seen the following type of practice foisted upon 6-and-under soccer players all too often:

- The practice begins with the coach having the players run a lap, without using balls, to warm up.
- Next, the coach leads the players in stretching exercises for 10 minutes.
- Stretching is followed by the deadliest line-up-and-wait-your-turn drill of them all, wherein the players dribble one at a time through a pattern of plastic cones before taking a shot at a goal.
- Next comes 10 minutes spent practicing sideline throw-ins.
- The coach calls a 5-minute water and snack break that invariably stretches to 10 minutes or longer while the coach visits with the players' parents.
- After the break, the coach spends 10 minutes lecturing on correct positioning for corner kicks while the players stand unmoving on the field.
- The practice ends with a 6-on-6 scrimmage during which the coach sets the young players in offensive and defensive positions and constantly stops play to make the young players return to those positions, where they stand around and do nothing while the ball is off somewhere else on the field.

Young soccer players don't enjoy the type of practice outlined above. (Nor do older players, for that matter.) When young players don't have fun at practice, they don't learn the game of soccer. Yet many coaches of young players employ some version of the above practice with their teams.

Why is that?

The answer lies in the fact that organized soccer leagues for young players are a relatively new phenomenon in America. (They don't even exist in other countries.) Until the publication of this book, coaches of young players could turn for guidance only to other soccer coaching books on the market—all of which were, and are, for coaching older players.

Moreover, because soccer wasn't offered to children 6 and younger when today's coaches of young players were that age, today's young-player coaches have had only their experiences as older players—generally in sports other than soccer—to fall back on. For the most part, those older-player experiences emphasized aspects of game play such as conditioning and strategy, as exemplified in the practice session above, that have little or nothing to do with helping 6-and-under players learn to play and love the game of soccer.

What aspects of soccer, then, *should* you emphasize with your team?

The answer lies in observing what the best players of the sport do, then applying that to your young players.

Controlled Touching

Think for a moment about any few minutes of professional soccer you've ever caught on television.

Did you see any goals scored?

Probably not.

Did you even see anyone take shots on goal?

Again, unless what you saw on television was a highlight reel, probably not. Instead, what you witnessed during just about any few minutes of live professional soccer was the ongoing battle between two teams fighting for position by crisply passing the ball from one teammate to another. That *battle for position*, similar to a football team on offense working its way down the field against a defense dedicated to stopping it, occupies most of every game of soccer.

But wait.

In the few minutes of the professional game you saw on television, did the players merely pass the ball back and forth to one another?

No.

Upon receiving a pass, each player *touched* the ball one to five times before passing it to another teammate. Those touches weren't for show. Rather, the player touched and moved the ball to gain the position necessary to make the next pass. The player's touches may have entailed dribbling around an opponent, moving forward, to the side, or even backward to get into position to make the desired pass.

At the same time, opponents constantly were trying to steal the ball, so the player's touches had to be made with *precision control*. This *controlled touching* of the ball is the single most critical skill required of all soccer players as they work as a team to win the battle for field position. Controlled touching is the heart and soul of soccer, and therefore it's the first—dare we say the only?—skill you need to teach your young players.

"Controlled touching is the heart and soul of soccer, and therefore it's the first—dare we say the only?—skill you need to teach your young players."

Simplicity Itself

There's a reason this book is simple and straightforward. That's because the game of soccer is simple and straightforward as well. Soccer is all about touching, moving, and passing the ball with the foot and body in fluid and creative ways.

And that's it.

How, then, to teach your players that basic truth?

By *not* running the sort of practice outlined at the beginning of this chapter. Rather, by running the practice sessions provided at the end of this book that are made up of a series of fun, touch-oriented drills that build one upon another.

The touch-oriented drills in this book are aimed at assuring that the players on your team touch the ball with their feet a theoretical thousand times during each practice session. Why? Because touching the ball with the foot at this young impressionable age is the key to becoming a good soccer player—and thus a player who enjoys the game of soccer—in the years ahead.

Just as young children's brains are hardwired to easily learn a second language, so too are their brains fully capable of learning the key element of soccer—touching and moving the ball with the foot. But they can do so only

The Term *Drills*

We use the term *drills* throughout this book to describe the various activities you'll use during your practice sessions to encourage your young players to touch and move the ball with their feet. We make use of the term simply to differentiate these practice activities from the weekly games, or matches, your team likely will play during the season.

In reality, the drills we present in this book are exciting games you'll play with your team throughout each practice. As such, you'll keep the idea of fun foremost in your young players' minds by making a point of always using the term *games* when describing and presenting these drills to your players. You'll have even more success with these drills when you present them to your young players in the form of *stories*. Suggested story lines for the drills you'll run with your players are offered with the descriptions of those drills.

if you give them the opportunity to *soak up* that knowledge—to *learn by doing*.

The practice session outlined at the beginning of this chapter gives young players virtually no opportunity to touch and move the ball with their feet. By contrast, the practice sessions detailed in this book and the drills around which those sessions are built provide young players with the opportunity to develop this all-important soccer skill, and to have fun while doing so.

You'll find the touch-oriented practice sessions we lay out in this book easy to run with your young players. Moreover, your players will enjoy practicing with you, and you with them, because the sessions encourage your players to do what they want to do—have fun kicking soccer balls around a field.

Too Easy?

But, you might be saying to yourself by now, aren't we making this whole thing sound a little *too* easy? After all, you're faced with the task of organizing a bunch of little kids and teaching them a game filled with enough nuances to challenge professional players who have devoted their entire lives to it.

In answer, we suggest you think of your young-player soccer coaching stint this way: most parents don't spend much time obsessing over how they're ever going to teach their children to talk. Rather, their children simply begin talking one day and learn to speak with ever-greater fluency as they grow up.

In much the same fashion, you needn't obsess over how you're going to teach your young players the game of soccer. When you use the methods detailed in this book to encourage your young players to have fun touching and moving the ball with their feet, your players' soccer skills will improve in the seasons and years ahead, just as their speaking skills have improved over the last few years from "ma-ma" and "pa-pa" to speaking in full sentences.

Competition

As important as it is to your young players for you to emphasize touching the ball, it's equally important to them for you to de-emphasize the competitive aspects of the game of soccer.

To understand why, picture playing a board game with a 4- or 5-year-old. Half the time it's impossible to convince the youngster to follow the rules. She'd much rather make up her own. Besides, she doesn't really have the attention span necessary to concentrate for an entire game. And if she *does* manage to finish the game, she'd better have been allowed to win.

A couple of years later, the same child will enjoy the same game, played competitively and by the rules, immensely.

The same difference in maturity levels holds true for soccer players who are 6 and younger versus those who are 7 and above. Disaster awaits you in the form of unhappy players and disgruntled parents if you don't take that difference into account. The simple truth is that if you coach your young players with older-player, competition-oriented techniques, most won't enjoy the game of soccer. Indeed, they may well reject the sport out of hand before they ever have the chance to truly get a feel for it.

Many times we've had experienced soccer coaches tell us how difficult they find it to step back from advanced soccer and teach the basics of the game to 7- through 10-year-olds. Yet for your players, who are even younger, you must step back even further. For example, you'll do a disservice to your young players if you so much as *mention* to them the concept of winning and losing their weekly games—the very basis of soccer and nearly every other sport.

Why is that?

"Kids learn by being spontaneous, creative, and by taking chances," notes child sports expert Bob Bigelow in *Just Let the Kids Play*. "Practices and games do not serve children's needs if they discourage those natural instincts and create fears about making mistakes."

By placing any emphasis whatsoever on competition and on winning and losing with your young players, you'll create in them the *fear of making mistakes* that might lead to their team losing its games. In so doing, you'll effectively stifle your players' spontaneous, risk-taking natures—the very natures that enable them to easily learn the game of soccer at a young age in the first place.

Rather than introduce soccer to your young players as the competitive game it is—and, for them, eventually will be—you must instead introduce soccer to your young players as something that is *just plain fun*. By using the touch-oriented, fun-focused practices and drills detailed in this book, you'll create young soccer players who have a great time every time they take the field, and who come to love the game of soccer and want to pursue it in the future.

Creativity and Positive Reinforcement

As you undertake the task of coaching your young players, it's worth noting that in the quote above from *Just Let the Kids Play*, child sports expert Bigelow places creativity front and center as one of the key ways children learn.

When people talk about great stars of any sport, they often say the player is someone who "makes things happen." A perfect example is found in American soccer star Freddy Adu. Soccer experts first noticed Adu's prodigious talents shortly after he moved to the United States from Ghana as a boy. By the time he was 12, Adu was widely known among American and international soccer cognoscenti. In 2004, at age 14, Adu turned pro, joining Major League Soccer's D.C. United team.

Throughout Adu's meteoric rise to stardom, no one commented on how well the young player stayed in his position on the field. No one mentioned that Adu did a great job of using both hands and keeping both feet on the ground when throwing a ball into play from the sidelines. Rather, it was Adu's ability to "make things happen" with a soccer ball that set him apart from all other soccer players his age, his ability to *create* while touching and moving the soccer ball on the field.

It's unlikely one of your players will grow up to be the next Freddy Adu. Still, your job is to give every one of your players the *opportunity* to do so, because in so doing, you'll provide your young players with the opportunity to grow up to be better, more creative *people* and, if not Freddy Adus, then at least better, more creative *soccer players*. You'll do that by nurturing your young players' creativity, by being constantly and relentlessly positive, by encouraging them to take chances, by keeping every aspect of your team's practices and games focused not on winning and losing but on having fun—and thus free of the *stifling fear of failure*.

Over and over again, child development experts point out that children require constant positive encouragement in order to continue to be creative. A case in point: Picture yourself in a roomful of kindergartners. Ask how many of them can sing. You'll be greeted by a sea of raised hands and maybe even a few off-key lines of "Twinkle, Twinkle Little Star."

Now picture yourself asking the same question of a roomful of fifth-graders.

How many raised hands will you see? A handful, maybe. Three, perhaps. Or two.

Why? By fifth grade, kids have learned the adult expectation of what it means to be a singer. As far as they're concerned, most can't meet that expectation.

As a coach, your goal is to make sure your players know they're good and capable soccer players, every single one of them. Because they all are.

Coed or Not Coed?

Q. Our local soccer league requires all 6-and-under teams to be coed. I'm not sure how great it's going to be to have my son learning the game of soccer with a bunch of girls. As for myself as a coach, I feel like I'm better with boys than girls. I'd rather just coach an all-boys team. Is there any justification for my concerns?

A. No. Most youth soccer leagues are divided into boys' and girls' teams at all ages these days. Even so, strength-related athletic abilities of boys and girls are fairly equal at the 6-and-under level.

If you feel you're better with boys than with girls, try looking at coaching a coed team as an opportunity for you to get better at working with girls.

CHAPTER 3

The Game of Soccer for Young Players

Quick Coaching Guide

There may be no more pleasing spectacle on earth than a soccer game between two teams of very young players.

The best 6-and-under soccer games are 3-on-3 with no goalkeepers.

Only the most basic soccer rules need apply to 6-and-under games.

New ideas such as dual-field games and academy coaching are invigorating 6-and-under soccer.

Soccer is nothing more than the use of all parts of players' bodies except arms and hands—but primarily players' feet—to move a ball into an opposing team's goal.

And that's it.

Field size is flexible. Goal size is variable. Ball size and type aren't critical. Game length is negotiable. Number of players on a side can be changed to suit teams' needs.

All of which is what helps make soccer the most popular game on earth.

Soccer can be, and often is, played barefoot using an old tennis ball on an uneven patch of bare dirt with pairs of rocks for goals. Indeed, from such humble conditions come some of the world's best soccer players.

The simplicity of soccer also is what makes the game so accessible to young players.

In the last chapter, you envisioned any few minutes of professional soccer you've seen on television. Now take a moment to picture the exact opposite: any little-kid soccer game you've ever seen.

Are you smiling yet?

There may be no more pleasing spectacle on earth than a soccer game between two teams of very young players. Talk about a simple, joyous, rampaging free-for-all. The kids chase the ball around in one big mass, making the game appear that which it is—chaos. When the ball comes to a stop, the players gather around it like a swarm of bees, their little legs flailing. When the ball squirts free of the swarm, the players take off after it once again.

In the course of most little-kid soccer games, players steal the ball from their teammates at will. They dribble the ball up the field the wrong way and shoot at their own goal.

This is *soccer?* Well, yes. This is *little-kid* soccer. To our way of thinking, it's the best soccer there is.

Soccer for Young Players

The 6-and-under rules for the soccer league in which you're coaching probably are set already. Most likely, the specified field size is small (25 yards by 20 yards or so) to accommodate more fields on a given patch of grass, and young players' short legs.

The rules also might specify that no goalkeepers are allowed. If you're lucky, the rules call for games involving only four players on a side. If you're very lucky, games are 3-on-3—that is, only three players on each side.

In 2004 the U.S. Youth Soccer Association, the largest youth soccer organization in the country, changed its rules to say that all its members should play 3-on-3 soccer, without goalkeepers, at the 6-and-under level. For ten years before that, 3-on-3 play had been a U.S. Youth Soccer recommendation, but not a specified rule.

U.S. Youth Soccer adopted additional new rules in 2004 aimed at better accommodating the needs of young soccer players all the way up to age 13. The new rules call for games involving fewer players on smaller fields—so-called small-sided soccer games—for all preteen players. Sam Snow, U.S. Youth Soccer's director of coaching education, has the job of traveling the country touting the association's rules for small-sided soccer.

As of 2004, Snow estimates, roughly half of all 6-and-under soccer leagues affiliated with U.S. Youth Soccer played games with no goalkeepers and either three or four players per side. With U.S. Youth Soccer's new rules ratcheting up what for the preceding decade was only a recommendation, Snow says he believes most leagues will switch quickly to small-sided soccer teams for 6-and-under players.

U.S. Youth Soccer's member leagues, as well as other leagues across the country, already have switched or will switch to small-sided soccer because, says Snow, the association's small-sided rules "make educational sense."

"The rules are based on the egocentric reality of the 5-year-old," Snow says. "As far as they're concerned, the world revolves around them. The fewer players on the field, the more they themselves get to play."

The association's 2004 rule modifications notwithstanding, many leagues across the country—including, perhaps, yours—still play 6-on-6 at the 6-and-under level. These outdated games generally include a pair of goalkeepers. One of those goalkeepers does not play soccer while the ball is at the other end of the field, where the other goalkeeper tries to grab the ball with his hands—exactly what you've worked so hard to train him *not* to do during your practices. An additional five players run around the field for each side. Those ten players, and sometimes more, are what traditionally have given little-kid soccer its distinctive *en masse* look.

Some 6-and-under soccer games still include goalkeepers, one of whom does not play soccer while the ball is at the other end of the field.

When leagues switch to U.S. Youth Soccer's recommended small-sided game play from 6-on-6 play, the number of players on the field for 6-and-under games is reduced by half. We wholeheartedly welcome U.S. Youth Soccer's small-sided rules for 6-and-under play. For the sake of young soccer players across the country, we look forward to the day when all 6-and-under soccer games are 3-on-3.

The 6-on-6 format at the 6-and-under level is what traditionally has given young-player soccer its distinctive *en masse* look.

To be sure, the fun for parents of watching a huge pack of little kids charging around a soccer field is diminished when 3-on-3 play is instituted. But believe us, even with only six players on the field at a time, there still are more than enough swarm-style masses during games to please parents.

The beauty of 3-on-3 soccer for 6-and-under players lies with the fact that, with a total of only six players on the field, those players have a much greater opportunity to touch the ball during their games than if twice as many players are on the field. When players touch the ball more, they have more fun. And as long as they have fun, they'll keep coming back to learn more soccer in subsequent seasons.

In addition to 3-on-3 play and no goalkeepers, U.S. Youth Soccer's rules now call for the use of small balls (known as #3 balls) during 6-and-

Wish List for Little-Kid Soccer Games

1. Small field
2. Large goals with no goalkeepers
3. Only three players on a side
4. Use of small (#3 size) ball

under practices and games rather than the larger, #4 size balls for junior players most commonly sold in chain stores.

Smaller, #3 balls are lighter, which means young players can move and control them more easily and kick them farther than #4 balls. Use of the smaller, #3 balls will enable your young players to be more successful at soccer—and thus enjoy the game more.

The association's rules call for the use of large goals for 6-and-under play. Through the elimination of goalkeepers from games combined with the continued use of large goals, U.S. Youth Soccer is encouraging coaches to put the emphasis on the fun of playing soccer by assuring that young players score lots of goals.

The primary concern voiced by opponents of 3-on-3 soccer for young players is coach availability. If leagues reduce the size of teams to the four to six players necessary to field a three-child team, they'll never be able to scare up enough coaches to cover the increased number of teams, argue opponents of 3-on-3 play.

U.S. Youth Soccer has a ready response: Don't reduce the size of teams at all. If anything, expand the size of teams, from the traditional eight or so players necessary to field a 6-on-6 team to ten or so players.

And what to do with those extra players given the 3-on-3 format?

Why, play two games at once, says U.S. Youth Soccer.

To which we say, *"Fantastic."*

U.S. Youth Soccer now officially recommends that 3-on-3 games (as well as 4-on-4 games for 7- and 8-year-olds) be played using what is known as

U-6 versus 6-and-Under Soccer

As you've probably gathered by now, we're not overly hung up on correct definitions for various soccer terms in this book when it comes to little-kid soccer. Instead, our focus is on how best to introduce the game of soccer, and the whole idea of competitive athletics, to young players.

That said, a quick explanation is in order of the U-this-number, U-that-number age-grouping notations used by soccer leagues and associations across America and around the world.

In a nutshell, the capital letter *U* in age-grouping notations stands for "Under," and the number following *U* refers to the age that players must be younger than on a specified date (generally July 31). For example, U-6 teams essentially are made up of kindergartners—players who have not turned 6 by the July 31 immediately preceding the season in which the players are participating, be it fall or spring. U-6 players will then turn 6 on their birthdays throughout the year (from August 1 to July 31) that they play on their U-6 teams.

Other leagues use grade designations—preschool, kindergarten, first grade, and so on—for purposes of making up teams. That way, children who have been held back or moved ahead a year in school may play on teams with their classmates.

We use the term *6-and-under* in this book to include all players age 6 or younger, regardless what age-grouping system their leagues use.

the dual-field method—two fields, side by side, with coaches and substitutes in between. (See illustration.) Players rotate from one field to the second field and then to the substitution area for a breather before beginning the rotation once again. Parents and other spectators, meanwhile, watch and cheer from the outer edges of the two fields.

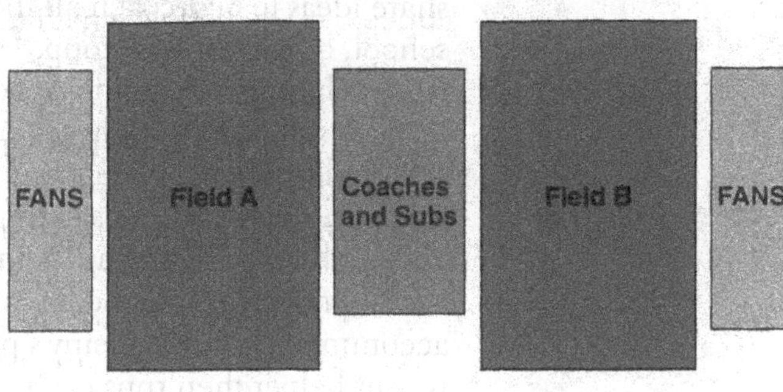

Dual-Field Game Format

Use of the dual-field method maximizes player participation, which is the key to young players having fun playing soccer.

Unfortunately, mention of the dual-field method is where opponents of U.S. Youth Soccer's rule that 6-and-under teams play 3-on-3 games—in other words, that little kids be allowed to play lots of soccer on their game days—really come unglued. How on earth, they opine, are they to coach two soccer games at once?

U.S. Youth Soccer answers with a brilliant *coup de grâce:* No one can coach two games at once.

"Just let the kids play soccer without all the grown-up interference, for crying out loud," says the association's Snow.

Okay, Snow didn't actually say the "for crying out loud" part. We just stuck it in there ourselves. But you catch the association's drift nonetheless.

(For detailed information on your role as a coach during games, see Chapter 7, Game Day.)

Academy Coaching

U.S. Youth Soccer's 6-and-under recommendations include another new coaching strategy, known as the "academy" method, for interested coaches of young players. We've used a variation of the strategy with great success over the years (though we didn't have a name for it until U.S. Youth Soccer released its recommendations).

U.S. Youth Soccer's recommended academy method seeks to replicate the idea of the sandlot or pickup sports games many of us played as children. The association's recommended method calls for several coaches to join forces to instruct a large number of 6-and-under players at once during single weekly gatherings that serve as both practices and games. On the selected day, the large group, or team, is divided into smaller groups, or squads. The squads then are run through various practice drills for 20 minutes or so. After a break, the squads scrimmage one another for another 20 minutes.

The academy method is great from a coaching standpoint because you and other coaches work together on behalf of your players. Experienced coaches offer advice to less experienced coaches, and you and other coaches share ideas to best coach all the same-aged players from your neighborhood, school, or league as a group.

Though U.S. Youth Soccer's academy method is highly laudable, most leagues still call for midweek practices followed by weekend games for 6-and-under players, as opposed to one combined practice/scrimmage each week. In response to this common league setup, we've developed a modified approach to the academy method.

Under our method, enough grids are set up for each weekly practice to accommodate the academy's players and coaches. One coach or recruited parent helper then runs each grid, wherein players perform one or two drills. Players rotate from grid to grid every 10 minutes, gaining the benefits of learning the game of soccer from several coaches. Coaches, meanwhile, benefit by being able to concentrate on presenting one or, at most, two drills throughout each practice. The larger group of players then splits up for game days (as detailed in answer to the following question).

Squad Assignments

Q. Two other coaches and I have joined forces to try the academy coaching method. Our group practices, with three teams' worth of players, have been great. Now it's time for our first game. The kids want to play on squads with their buddies. We were thinking of dividing up our team so that each of us coaches a squad made up of our respective daughters and their closest friends. But now we're wondering: Should we set up permanent squads for all our games this season?

A. No. Admittedly, it's easier to assign your players to a single squad and leave it at that for the entire season. The problem with doing so is that you unavoidably will create stronger and weaker squads no matter how carefully you split up your players. To knowingly assign players to weaker or stronger squads for an entire season is unfair.

We've developed an approach to the academy method of squad assignments that we highly recommend. We assign each player on our academy roster a number; then we form squads by different number groupings for each game. Such numbering schemes are infinite—odd and even numbers, every third number, etc. The key is to make up your squads differently for every single game throughout the season. That way players are constantly shifted from playing on squads that happen to be strong to squads that happen to be weak, and from playing with their best friends to playing with teammates they don't know well—and who might well become their best friends.

This approach of rotating squads keeps players from forming cliques. Better yet, it eliminates any creeping interschool or inter-neighborhood competitiveness that might otherwise arise through the creation of set, season-long squads.

As coaches, we've always worked to put the needs of our players before the wants of our players' parents (just as you should). Even so, it's worth reporting that over the years, our rotating-squad approach has been welcomed and supported by the parents of every single one of our players.

One final point: Be sure to determine squad assignments for the entire season and distribute sheets denoting those assignments to parents as soon as your academy's roster is set. That way parents will know their children's game times as early in the season as possible.

Continuing to Limit Player Numbers

As young players grow older, their advancing skills are addressed through U.S. Youth Soccer's 2004 rule changes specifying numbers of players on the field for games, just as their beginning skills are addressed by the rule changes. For players up to age 8 (or up to U-8), U.S. Youth Soccer calls for 4-on-4 games, still with small, #3 balls, no goalkeepers, and large goals.

Not until the 10-and-under age group (U-10) does U.S. Youth Soccer call for 6-on-6 play with goalkeepers and the use of larger, #4 size balls.

U.S. Youth Soccer's "grow-the-game" rules include gradually larger fields for each age group as well.

Player numbers continue to increase gradually as players grow even older. The association's rules call for 6-on-6 games for 10-and-under players and 8-on-8 games for players up to age 12. Not until players reach their teens does U.S. Youth Soccer call for 11-on-11 games. (Before releasing its new rules, U.S. Youth Soccer called for 11-on-11 games—the same as adult games—beginning at age 10.)

The association points out the obvious. Small-sided soccer games—those with fewer players on the field than in the past—make the game of soccer a better experience for all preteen players. During small-sided games, players gain what you, as coach, work so hard to ensure your players accomplish during practices—more touches on the ball. Those touches translate into more opportunities for players to make decisions about what to do with the ball when it's in their possession. Moreover, those decisions are less complicated—and therefore more age-appropriate—because there are fewer players on the field for the player with the ball to think about.

Still wondering about the wisdom of small-sided soccer for your 6-and-under players? Consider the sport of basketball. How many full 5-on-5 basketball games do kids play? Very few. Rather than wait for ten kids to show up before they take the court, children naturally play 1-on-1, 2-on-2, or 2-on-1 pickup basketball games all the time. As a result, they handle the ball more often and become better players more quickly than if they played only 5-on-5 games.

Inevitably, players in small-sided soccer games—as in small-sided basketball games—spend more time playing a better brand of soccer than in games involving more players. And that explains why the national youth soccer organizations of such soccer-powerhouse countries as England, Ireland, Germany, France, and Korea, among many others, now endorse the small-sided-game concept along with U.S. Youth Soccer.

A 6-and-Under Soccer Primer

In the same way the U.S. Youth Soccer Association now calls for gradually adding more players to the game as players grow older, so too are the rules of soccer gradually increased and enforced during soccer games as players grow older.

For your 6-and-under players, only the most necessary rules should be enforced. According to U.S. Youth Soccer, those worth enforcing include the following.

Scoring Goals

Scoring goals is the absolute highlight of little-kid soccer games, for players and parents alike.

A big part of U.S. Youth Soccer's small-sided-game modifications are aimed at increasing the ability of young players to advance the ball up the field, attack a large unguarded goal, and score more goals than in the past. That's because the more goals 6-and-under players score during their games, the more fun they have.

For that reason, U.S. Youth Soccer recommends the use of unguarded goals as large as 18 feet wide by 6 feet high for 6-and-under soccer games. In fact, according to the association's 6-and-under recommendations, goals can be eliminated entirely and a score counted each time a team pushes the ball across the end line it is attacking. (We don't recommend eliminating goals, however, as there is nothing more fun for young players than watching their shots go into the net for a score.)

A goal is scored when the entire ball passes beyond the entire line marking the entry to the goal as demarcated by the arms and crossbar of the goal, as long as the ball has not been propelled into the goal by an offensive player's hand or arm.

Each goal equals one point for the scoring team.

Out-of-Bounds

The out-of-bounds rule is nothing more than a necessary evil at the 6-and-under level of play.

Many experienced coaches of young players avoid using sidelines at all, preferring that their players continue playing soccer as much as possible rather than having the flow of their game interrupted by sideline throw-ins. When the ball wanders too far astray, a coach who favors this approach simply nabs the ball and heaves it back toward the center of the field, with the players streaming along behind it.

Such a tactic doesn't work during official games, when spectators are gathered near the sidelines. At those times, it'll be necessary to enforce the out-of-bounds rule, at least loosely.

The out-of-bounds rule states that the ball is out-of-bounds only when the entire ball is beyond the entire boundary line. One way you can keep your team playing soccer as much as possible during games is to attempt to keep spectators a few feet back from the sidelines and end lines and to encourage loose enforcement of the out-of-bounds rule by the referee. In many cases, young players will attempt to keep the ball in play as they near and cross the out-of-bounds line with the ball. This is great practice at ball control and should be allowed as much as possible.

As long as the ball, even though clearly out-of-bounds by as much as a foot or so, is still being played and is in the process of being herded back onto the playing field, and as long as the players aren't being constricted by onlookers, you may want to have the referee encourage players with a friendly shout to keep playing. Only when the ball goes squirting far off the field must the referee halt the game so the ball may be returned to play with a kick-in or throw-in.

Kick-Ins versus Throw-Ins

If we and U.S. Youth Soccer have our way, sideline throw-ins by young players—a bane of all young-player coaches—soon will be a thing of the past.

Two problems are inherent in having your young players perform sideline throw-ins to restart play when the ball has gone out-of-bounds after last being kicked or touched by a member of the opposing team:

1. During practice, you'll spend all your time coaching your players to use their feet while playing soccer. Suddenly trying to get them to use their hands for one particular aspect of the game will confuse them. Sideline throw-ins thus will detract from your efforts to emphasize having your players move and control the ball with their feet as much as possible.
2. In the same way 6-and-under youngsters don't yet have the hand-eye coordination necessary to throw a baseball or football well, so too are they incapable of performing sideline throw-ins well. As a result, 6-and-under soccer games routinely are stymied, delayed, halted, and almost ruined by well-meaning referees who interrupt play to make young players repeat throw-ins that often go backward or straight up in the air, or that travel only a few feet.

   Even when a ball is thrown out into the field of play with adequate force and in the correct direction, well-meaning referees often stop play unnecessarily to have the player repeat the throw-in because she didn't perform it correctly. There's no reason to waste young players' valuable soccer playing time to practice sideline throw-ins. As a coach, you should do what you can to ensure it doesn't occur.

A correct, by-the-rules throw-in entails the player throwing the ball straight over the top of the head, using both hands equally, while keeping both feet on the ground and entirely outside the field of play. The throw-in is performed from the spot where the ball left the field of play after last being touched by a member of the opposing team.

Rather than use sideline throw-ins during games, however, U.S. Youth Soccer recommends 6-and-under players be directed to place the ball on the ground at the point along the sideline where the ball went out, and to kick it back into the game from there. This substitution of kick-ins for throw-ins is a perfect solution to the problems associated with 6-and-under sideline throw-ins.

You'll help your players by suggesting adoption of U.S. Youth Soccer's kick-in recommendation in your 6-and-under league. If your league's officials aren't ready to agree to such a change, you may want to circumvent their old-school ways by visiting with the coach of each of your opposing teams, on a game-by-game basis, and suggesting the use of kick-ins rather than throw-ins by players on both teams. (If rule circumvention isn't in your nature, simply relax and enjoy watching your players' efforts at throwing in the ball correctly during your games.)

Duration

Adult and older-kid soccer games are divided into two halves. However, most soccer leagues understand and abide by young players' need for more frequent breaks. As a result, 6-and-under soccer games generally are divided into quarters, with short breaks for a breather and a quick drink of water after the first and third quarters, and a longer halftime break for water and perhaps a piece of fruit.

Note that your team shouldn't switch goals with the opposing team after halftime. It's difficult enough for 6-and-under players to figure out which goal to shoot at as it is. There's no need to confuse them further.

For 6-and-under players, U.S. Youth Soccer recommends 8-minute quarters with 2-minute breaks between quarters and a 5-minute halftime break. If you and the opposing team both have plenty of players, you might be able to push the lengths of quarters to 10 minutes—assuming your opposing coach is agreeable—to maximize the amount of time your players have fun playing soccer on game day.

Refereeing

Referees are virtually unnecessary in 6-and-under soccer games, especially small-sided, 3-on-3 games where the players pretty much run things themselves.

Very rarely are fouls by 6-and-under players purposeful. Any rule infringements—usually, a kid who is confusing soccer with tackle football—need simply be explained briefly to the offending player, preferably with play continuing. Do-overs or allowing play to continue when such infractions occur should be the rule rather than taking the ball away from one team and awarding possession to the other. Penalizing a player simply creates uncertainty for all the young players on the field. Remember, instead of getting caught up in handing out discipline, the idea is to encourage success for all the young players in the game.

One crucial time the referee should stop play is when a player falls near the ball amid a mass of players, their kicking feet flying. In this instance, the referee should call off play. Once the fallen player has gotten up, play should resume with the team last in possession kicking the ball.

Little hands invariably reach out to stop the flight of balls that are kicked into the air during 6-and-under games. Referees should simply let such infractions pass without comment and without halting play to award a free kick to the opposing side. However, every now and then a hand ball infraction is so blatant that players stop the game of their own accord with the ball lying at the feet of the offending player. In such a case, it'll be up to the referee to quickly restart play by awarding possession via a free kick to the opposing team. During free kicks, opposing players must stand at least 4 yards away from the ball until it is kicked.

Whistles for use by referees—and their negative connotations—are unnecessary at the 6-and-under level and should not be used. The general rule of thumb should be to let the kids play their games on their own, without adult interference, as much as possible.

(For more on refereeing 6-and-under players, see pages 60–62.)

Goal Kicks

A goal kick consists of the ball being kicked up the field after being placed on the ground within or at the edge of the goal box by either the goalkeeper

Definition: Goal Box

The goal box is a small rectangular box painted on the field in front of the goal. The goalkeeper or another player from the team must execute goal kicks from within this box.

It's worth noting that 6-and-under players attacking a goal often stop at the edge of the goal box if one is painted on the field. They needn't do so. They may, if they wish, run all the way into the goal while dribbling the ball in order to score a goal.

There's nothing wrong and everything right with encouraging this sort of aggressive play with your young players as a way of encouraging their dribbling skills early on in their soccer careers. In fact, as a way to reinforce the importance of keeping the ball close as players dribble it, we've even gone so far as to tell our young players that the "best" goals are those in which our players actually enter the goal themselves while kicking the ball. You may wish to tell your players the same thing.

or a defensive player. A goal kick is taken when the ball is knocked out-of-bounds over the end line by an opposing player.

The concept of goal kicks by young players is simplified when goalkeepers are not used. When such is the case, U.S. Youth Soccer recommendations call for goal kicks to be taken by any player. Rather than take the kick from within the goal box, which needn't even be painted on the field for games with no goalkeepers, the association recommends that the ball simply be placed a few yards back into the field of play, in line with where it crossed the end line. A player then kicks the ball back into play from there.

During goal kicks, opposing players must stand at least 4 yards away from the ball until it is kicked.

Corner Kicks

Corner kicks are yet another potential point of confusion for young players.

When the ball rolls out-of-bounds over the end line of the defending team after last being touched by a defending player, the attacking team is awarded a corner kick. A corner kick is taken, as the name suggests, from the corner of the field nearest where the ball went out-of-bounds. Any player from the attacking team may set the ball anywhere within or on the lines of the small corner arc in each corner of the field and kick it back into play from there. Defending players must stand at least 4 yards away until the ball is kicked.

It takes a year or two for most young players to understand the concept of corner kicks. In the meantime, whoever acts as referee for your 6-and-under games will need to help out with corner kicks by setting the ball in the corner arc and explaining which team is to kick the ball and perhaps even directing particular players to take each kick.

Substitutions

As players grow older, the rules governing the number of substitutions allowed per game and when substitutions may be made are instituted—generally beginning when players reach age 10 or so.

For your 6-and-under players, no rules about substitutions need apply. You should feel free to substitute your players in and out of games, while play is ongoing, at will. Substitution may be necessary in the following circumstances:

A *player on the field is obviously growing tired and is unable to keep up with the other players.*

In such a situation, you should send in a substitute and have the tired player get a drink and maybe spend a minute or two in the lap of his parent. Then get the player back over near you, ready to return to the game.

A player becomes overly rambunctious on the field.

There is a fine line between fun yet aggressive play by 6-and-under players and play so rough that other players or the offending player may get hurt.

Six-and-under players don't have the body coordination necessary to engage in the kinds of contact allowed in older-kid soccer games. Instead, it'll be up to you to explain to your players that, for the time being, their brand of soccer is of the noncontact variety.

You should send in a substitute for any player on your team who is tripping, kicking, bumping, tackling, or elbowing other players. (Note: In his rush to reach and kick the ball, such a player is as likely to engage in such contact with the players on his own team as with players on the opposing team.) You can then explain to the player how he should comport himself on the field when it's his turn to return to the game. Short stints on the sideline encourage such youngsters to better control their rambunctiousness while remaining fun-loving, aggressive players.

A player is injured.

The vast majority of injuries during 6-and-under games fall into the "ouchie" category. In such cases, when a player comes limping off the field with tears in her eyes, you'll need to send in a substitute right away. Then you can have the "injured" player spend a few minutes in the lap of her parent before encouraging her to return to the sideline with the rest of the substitute players, ready to return to play.

If your league insists on using goalkeepers at the 6-and-under level, expect that a number of your players will have the wind knocked out of them by shots taken to the midsection by balls kicked at them from close range. Such gut shots are scary, with the struck player collapsing to the ground clutching his stomach. You'll need to jog to the injured player and help him off the field to his parent, where he can have a drink while getting his wind back. Generally he'll be ready to head back out onto the field of play—though probably not as goalkeeper—within a few minutes.

If an injured player chooses not to return to the game at all, that's fine. Just let her know how much you appreciate what she did for the team up to that point, and encourage her to relax with her teammates along the sidelines until the end of the game.

With regard to substitutions, your goal should be for all your players to play equal amounts of each game, and for all your players to play, at minimum, 50 percent of each game.

Other Rules

The game of soccer for older players is governed by many more rules than those covered here. As a 6-and-under coach, you needn't worry about them yet. If, however, you want to learn more about the many rules that will govern your players' games in the years ahead—including fouling, tackling the ball, offside, and penalty kicks—visit the U.S. Youth Soccer Association's website, www.usyouthsoccer.org.

Fighting for Your Players

Q. The league in which I'm a coach calls for 6-and-under soccer games to include goalkeepers and playing six players on a side, with up to 8-on-8 allowed. Should I fight for the elimination of goalkeepers and a reduction in player numbers?

A. Absolutely. Remember, you'll be fighting the good fight for the benefit of your players. Be forewarned, however: you may well meet stiff opposition from the powers-that-be in your league.

That said, soccer leagues across the country increasingly are adopting U.S. Youth Soccer's small-sided-game rules for 6-and-under games. Your players will be the direct beneficiaries if you launch an ultimately successful bid to convince your league's officials to make their—and your—league the next to adopt the association's rules.

When making your pitch to your league, use U.S. Youth Soccer's detailed information about the benefits of small-sided teams and games. Go to www.usyouthsoccer.org and click on the Coaches link, then click on "Small-Sided Games Resource Center" under Related Topics, and then on the "Why Small-Sided Games" article.

Off the Field

Quick Coaching Guide

As coach, it's up to you to manage the expectations of your players' parents.

Be sure to delegate all off-field duties to your players' parents so you can concentrate on coaching.

Select and make full use of a parent helper.

Appropriately celebrating the end of each season with your young players may be the most important—and rewarding—aspect of your role as coach.

You'll do much to set yourself and your players up for a good season of soccer if you spend a little time thinking through and taking care of a handful of off-the-field details before the season begins.

Managing Parents' Expectations

Perhaps no part of your job as coach is more important to you and your young players than managing the expectations of your players' parents. From the get-go, it's critical that you emphasize your coaching philosophy and the reasoning behind it to the parents of your players.

You'll want to emphasize the following key points:

- Young players learn the basics of soccer best by having lots of fun touching and moving the ball with their feet.
- Practices are important as learning opportunities while having fun; games are for players to show off their team shirts, chase around after the ball, enjoy after-game treats, and simply have a good time.
- Six-and-under players are not yet ready for the win-lose aspects of competitive game play. You'll de-emphasize the idea of winning and losing games with your players, and you'll expect parents to do the same by, for

example, asking their children after their games whether they had fun, not whether they won or lost.

- During games, you'll equalize playing time for all players. More advanced players will spend as much time on the sidelines as less advanced players.
- Team members who aren't quite ready for the melee of games needn't play. If they want to sit on the sidelines and watch, that's fine. If they don't even want to show up on game day, that's fine, too.
- Team members who don't wish to practice are welcome to watch from the sidelines as well—for the entire season or longer if that's what it takes for them to grow comfortable with the idea of joining their teammates on the field.
- The rare team member who doesn't want to participate in practices but wants to play on game day will be allowed to do so. In years ahead when practices involve tactical preparation for games, practice attendance will, of necessity, be a prerequisite for game play. But your 6-and-under players aren't at that point yet. Your goal is simply to encourage your team members to have fun playing soccer. Whether they do so only during practices or only during games—or neither for a while—is not important.
- Parents should offer only positive encouragement to their children and other players during practices and games.

A two-part approach to the critically important job of expressing your 6-and-under coaching philosophy to your players' parents works well.

First, track down the e-mail addresses of your team's parents. Your soccer league most likely will be able to provide you with that information. Send your own, personalized version of an introductory letter to parents based on the sample provided here (see opposite). Your letter should be e-mailed to parents a week or two prior to your team's first practice. Use the phone or postal service if you don't have a parent's e-mail address.

Second, gather the parents at the start of your first practice and quickly go through the main points of your letter with them. Your willingness to put voice to your philosophy lets the parents know you're serious about your beliefs. As such, your addressing these issues will go a long way toward ending problems with parents of your players before those problems ever crop up.

Overall, clarity to the point of bluntness is not a bad thing when it comes to managing parent expectations. In fact, the clearer you are with parents, the more you'll find they appreciate your forthrightness, and the more inclined they'll be to respect your philosophy and to follow your lead in making sure your young players—their children—have a great season by having lots of fun playing soccer.

Delegating Parental Duties

Once you've clarified your coaching philosophy with your players' parents, your next step will be to delegate duties to them.

Sample Letter on Coaching Philosophy

Dear Parents:

I'm looking forward to coaching your child this season.

My coaching efforts will be based on a coaching philosophy geared to the needs of the young players on our team. I'd appreciate your help in reinforcing that philosophy with your child.

- Please join me in offering only positive encouragement to your child and other team members throughout the season.
- I'll emphasize fun foremost during practices by teaching a few basic ball-control skills through energetic practice activities that will encourage players to touch and move the ball with their feet as much as possible.
- I won't worry about whether our team "wins" or "loses" the games it plays this season. I hope you won't either.
- All team members will be offered equal playing time during games.
- Players not quite ready to join in on the field during games are welcome to watch from the sidelines or not attend games at all.
- Players not quite ready to join in during practices are likewise welcome to watch from the sidelines until they're ready, even if the process takes more than one season.
- Players who aren't ready to participate in practices but want to participate in games are welcome to do so.

I look forward to meeting you and your child at our team's first practice, which will be held at *time and place.*

Sincerely,

Your Name and Contact Information

Remember, your primary task is plenty challenging: to introduce the sport of soccer—and, in most cases, the whole idea of competitive athletics—to a group of very young children. You *must* put your energies into your coaching duties on the field. That means delegating *all* off-field duties to your players' parents—and we do mean *delegate.*

Duties (detailed later in this chapter) that you'll need to ensure are handled by your players' parents include the following:

- Supplying fruit slices, water, and paper cups for players at halftime during games
- Supplying end-of-game treats and drinks
- Organizing the end-of-season celebration, including the production of player awards
- Most important, but often most difficult to accomplish, enlisting the support of a parent helper during practices—assuming your team, like most, has between seven and twelve members

We recommend delegating the first three of the four duties listed above via a handout (see below) at your team's first practice. This handout—which should be given directly to parents, not entrusted to your young players—should include the following:

- A quick, one- or two-sentence reiteration of your coaching philosophy and parent expectations as a way to continue pounding your message home
- A list of what players should wear and bring to practices and games (see pages 37–39 for details)
- Team roster (with phone numbers so parents can call one another to trade assigned duties if necessary)

Sample Handout for the First Practice

Greetings:

We're ready to start a great season of soccer together. During the season we'll emphasize learning basic ball-control skills by having lots of fun playing soccer. Our team's young players will have a successful season if we:

1. Emphasize fun rather than winning and losing;
2. Understand that every player will be offered equal playing time for every game; and
3. Make sure our comments are always positive and encouraging.

Here's what your child will need for every practice and game:

- Team shirt
- Shorts, sweats, or loose pants
- Cleats (cannot be metal)
- Shin guards held in place by long socks (Players *must* wear these for every practice and game to avoid injury. Please be sure your child's footwear, shin guards, and socks fit well and are comfortable.)
- Small, #3 size soccer ball (Worth purchasing for your child's use over the next couple of years because #3 balls are lighter and easier for young players to use than the larger, more common #4 size balls. By using a #3 size ball, your child will have more fun and learn more soccer.)
- Water bottle and snack

Please see the three attached sheets:

1. Team roster with contact information
2. Practice and game schedule
3. Assignments for providing halftime snacks (fruit slices, water, paper cups), end-of-game treats and drinks, and end-of-season celebration treats (cake or cupcakes and drink)

Thanks!

Your Name and Contact Info

- Practice and game schedule
- A list of assigned parent duties

For each game, we suggest you assign one player's parents to provide, for the entire team, a halftime snack of fruit slices and water in paper cups. Assign another player's parents the task of providing an end-of-game treat and drink. (Note that you'll be asking all parents to provide water and snacks for their kids at games, as well as assigning specific parents to provide half-time fruit and water, and end-of-game treats and drinks. That redundancy is purposeful; your players will benefit from your efforts to assure they are well fed and hydrated on game days.) We also recommend that you assign one or two parents the task of bringing treats and drinks to the end-of-season celebration to be held right after your team's final game. (For more on the end-of-season celebration and awards, see pages 34–36.) Of course, it'll be up to you to distribute parent duties as evenly as possible.

Be sure to note on the assignment list that parents who are unable to attend games at which they're expected to provide halftime snacks or end-of-game treats should trade duties with other parents. There's no need to have parents who trade duties with one another inform you of their trades.

Recruiting a Parent Helper

Recruiting a parent helper is a bit trickier than the three parent duties we've already discussed. Those you can just delegate; this one you must finesse a bit. It is, however, by far the most critical of the duties you'll need help with.

Given the young ages of your players and their short attention spans, you can't do a good job if you coach more than six players at once during practices. Instead, if your practices with your 6-and-under players are to be successful—are to be fun, and not dissolve into chaos—you'll need to run your practice-session drills with no more than six players at a time.

In the unlikely event your team has six or fewer players, you'll be able to coach your entire team yourself. If, however—as is much more likely—you have between seven and twelve players on your team, you'll need to set up two separate practice grids and recruit a parent to help out during practices. If—gulp—you have thirteen to eighteen players on your team and you're the only coach, you'll need to set up *three* grids and recruit *two* parent helpers.

Recruiting a parent helper is actually easier than you might at first imagine. If, before the start of the season, you can recruit a parent helper who shares your coaching philosophy, great. If not, go into your first practice knowing that, at the 6-and-under level, most parents stick around for the duration of their children's practices. Many will be dealing with younger siblings of the players. Others likely will be hanging out, perhaps talking on a cell phone or chatting with another parent, but more or less available to help. Those parents are your marks.

When you have all the parents gathered before you at the start of your first practice, request that a parent help you out "just for this one practice." Pause and let adult peer pressure work its magic on your marks. After a moment's hesitation, one of the parents will grudgingly offer to help. You can then set up the parent to run drills with half the players on your team.

Our experience has been that when parents help out for one practice, they discover it's much more fun to play soccer with a bunch of little kids than it is to sit on the sidelines looking on, and they're anxious to help for the rest of the season. If, however, your first recruit clearly isn't interested in helping again, recruit another parent at the next practice and, if necessary, another at the next, until you find a parent who has fun running drills with the team and is happy to assist you by running a practice grid for the rest of the season.

You may want to photocopy from this book the drills your parent helper will be running for you in practice and give them to your helper—provided you're sure doing so won't make your helper feel unduly "official" and scare her away. Likewise, you may want to pass this book on to your parent helper if she is particularly gung ho about helping out.

Remember that even though you've recruited a parent helper, you're still the coach; you still run the practices. Your helper simply enables you to keep the practices organized and the players playing soccer rather than standing around waiting their turn.

Note, too, that it's your responsibility to assure that your parent helper shares your philosophy, and so remains unfailingly positive and de-emphasizes winning and losing. In the unlikely event that your parent helper turns out to be negative or overly competitive, it's your job to discuss the situation with the parent helper—and it's your job to find a replacement for him if he continues his negative or overly competitive ways.

You *must* replace a poor parent helper, even at the risk of angering the parent and possibly losing that parent's child from your team. Remember, your responsibility to the mental well-being of all your players and to their futures as soccer players *must* come before any concerns you may have about what any one of your players' parents may think of you.

The End-of-Season Celebration

Appropriately celebrating the end of each season with your young players may well be the single most important—and rewarding—aspect of your role as coach. Here's why: Running a celebration correctly can go a long way toward assuring your young players that they're great kids and their participation in the sport of soccer is a terrific thing.

Over time, we've developed a successful end-of-season celebration that's simple, straightforward, and fun for everyone.

Many teams schedule the end-of-season celebration for a separate time and date after the season is over. Such a celebration often involves meeting at a park or someone's home for a potluck picnic or supper. Invariably, given the busy schedules of most families these days, as many as half the players and their parents will not attend the celebration.

Instead, to encourage full participation in what, if handled correctly, is such an important component of your team's season, we suggest that you schedule the end-of-season celebration immediately following the final game of the season right at the playing field. To further encourage full participation, schedule an unofficial team photo opportunity—a chance for parents to snap away with their personal cameras—for the same time and place.

At the beginning of the season, assign two sets of parents with the job of bringing drinks and a cake or cupcakes to the celebration. Once the final game ends, have all your players gather near the treats (though not so near that they are overly tempted by them). Before breaking into the cake and drinks, it'll be up to you to perform the simple ceremony that is the heart of the end-of-season celebration.

Have your players sit at your feet with their parents standing behind them. Then, one at a time, have each player stand in front of you, facing her teammates. Using remarks prepared in advance, say a sentence or two about each player—about what makes her, in particular, an especially valuable member of the team as a whole.

Then present that player with a personalized token of your and your team's appreciation for her season-long participation. That token can be a computer-generated certificate signed by you as coach. (We ask a computer-savvy parent to produce the certificates for our players. The certificates generally are designed around the theme of the team name chosen by our players at the beginning of the season.)

The certificates you present might read something like this: "In Great Appreciation for an Outstanding Contribution to the Cheetahs, Fall 2005, This Certificate of Participation Is Hereby Granted to *player's name*." Any wording of that sort is fine, as is simply the player's name, season date, team name, and your signature. The important thing is that your players receive certificates—and the more flowery and impressive looking they are, the better.

By far the most enjoyable moment you'll likely have as a coach will be when you lean forward to present the certificates to your players and catch, for just a second, the look of complete pride and happiness that fills each player's face and lights up each player's eyes as his teammates and parents cheer wildly for him. That magical moment, repeated for every player, is what makes the end-of-season celebration so critical and what ends each player's season so appropriately. It's guaranteed to bring tears to your eyes, and to the eyes of your players' parents as well.

Only after the certificates are handed out and the team pictures are taken should you break out the cake and drinks.

Trophies

Q. What about giving my players trophies?

A. As with so many overdone things in American life, today's young athletes, regardless of sport, are so inundated with trophies that, in many cases, receipt of trophies has come to mean less to them than it might if they received trophies less often.

We recommend not presenting trophies to your young players every season. Instead, we have found the personalized certificates, as described above, to be perfectly acceptable for young players.

That said, there's no question that kids *do* love trophies. In response, we have found that trophies presented to players after they have been together as a team for a couple of years makes a good compromise.

If you're going to present your players with trophies, the key to making them become lifelong keepsakes, we've learned, is to personalize them. That doesn't just mean having each player's name inscribed on her trophy. Rather, we have found that naming each and every player "best" at something and having that "best" attribute inscribed on the trophy along with the player's name is what makes receiving a trophy truly special.

It doesn't really matter what, exactly, you declare each player best at. Rather, it's the fact that you've declared each and every one of your players best at something that will fill all of them with fully justifiable pride.

Assuming your team isn't overly large, you should have no problem coming up with a "best" that is personalized and specific to each of your players. In fact, we successfully came up with individual "bests" for our team of twenty-one players one season. Examples to get you started include "Best Ball Handler," "Best Dribbler," "Best Ball Mover," "Best Kicker," "Best Attacker," "Best Ball Stealer," "Best Striker," and so on.

As with the presentation of the certificates described above, the key when presenting trophies is to get each player up in front of his peers and parents while you offer a sentence or two describing exactly why that player is best at whatever you've deemed him best at. Then lean forward and enjoy taking note of the wonderfully proud look on your player's face as you hand him his trophy.

CHAPTER 5

On the Field

Quick Coaching Guide

Your players' equipment needs are minimal but important.

The only truly critical piece of "equipment" you need to bring to practice is the right attitude.

Helping your players choose their team name is an important part of your duties as a 6-and-under coach.

Okay. You've taken care of your parent management needs and have delegated parent duties. It's time to get ready to take the field with your team.

Your Players' Equipment Needs

Here's what your players need to wear or bring to every practice and game, and why they need to have it.

Team Jersey

You'll likely never reach full compliance among the parents of your players with getting your players to wear their team shirts to practice, but getting close is good enough. Young players are enthralled with the idea of playing on a *team*. Having your players wear their team shirts to practices in addition to games gives them more opportunities to feel the pride of being a part of something bigger than themselves. That's heady as well as healthy stuff for 6-and-under kids.

If the team shirts your league uses are reversible, so much the better. Having your players switch their shirt colors as necessary during practices will save your having to buy and use mesh bibs for the same purpose. Girls will need to wear T-shirts beneath their team shirts in order to reverse their shirts without any potential embarrassment.

Shorts, Sweats, or Loose Pants

There's no need for you to insist on shorts at this age, and certainly no need to insist on soccer-specific shorts. Sweats or loose long pants are fine for your young players, especially on cold days.

Cleats

Young players benefit as much as older players from the added traction they gain by wearing cleats when they play soccer, especially on wet fields.

To avoid injuries to other players, cleats must be made entirely of plastic or rubber, not metal.

Inexpensive multisport cleats from chain stores are fine at this age. Your players don't need expensive, brand-name soccer cleats—not for a few more years anyway.

Shin Guards

To minimize the most common 6-and-under "ouchie," kicked and bruised shins, insist that all your players wear shin guards for every practice and game.

We have found that blaming the sponsoring soccer league and lawyers works well as a way to get parents to outfit their children with shin guards. "The league insists on them," we tell parents. "It's the lawyers. What can we say? Our hands are tied."

Shin guards should be covered by long socks to hold them in place. Whether the long socks are true soccer socks doesn't matter. If shin guards

If shin guards aren't held in place, players may end up with well-protected calves — and shins just waiting to be kicked.

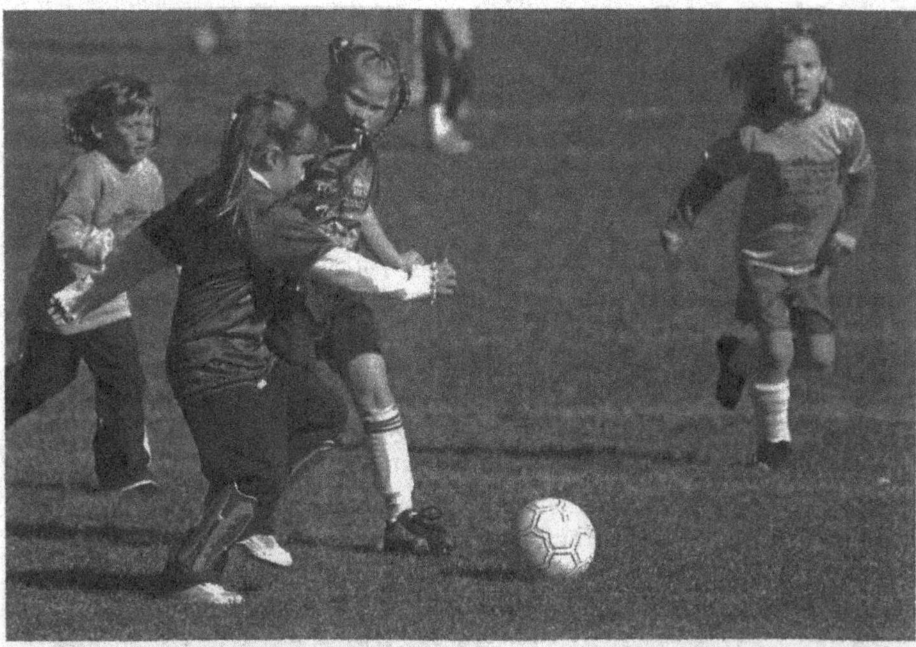

aren't held in place, they tend to slip around backward until players are running around the field with well-protected calves and unprotected shins just waiting to be kicked.

It's not unusual for youngsters to refuse to practice or play in a game, or to play halfheartedly, simply because their footwear, shin guards, or socks are uncomfortable. If you suspect some of your players are experiencing this problem, alert their parents.

Small, #3 Size Soccer Ball

Players will need a #3 size soccer ball. Chain department stores are just beginning to carry #3 balls. The small balls long have been available online and in chain sporting goods stores and specialty soccer shops.

Your players will benefit greatly from your insistence that parents obtain #3 balls for them. Proportion-wise, the small balls fit your players' smaller bodies. The lighter balls are therefore easier for your young players to move, control, and kick. As a result, players who use #3 balls will have greater success on the field and more fun playing soccer than those who use larger balls.

Full Water Bottle

This is another area in which you'll have difficulty reaching full compliance. Some of your players' parents likely won't yet understand the important role good hydration plays in the health and well-being of their young athletes. That's why, after being as gently insistent as possible that parents send water with their children to practices and games, you may want to provide water yourself at practices, as noted later in this chapter.

Snack

Suggest that your players eat a small snack before practice begins if they wish. During your short practice sessions, stop only to take quick water breaks, not longer snack breaks.

You might want to pass on to parents two additional notes regarding player equipment:

- With so many soccer players starting out at such a young age in this country, small-sized cleats, shin guards, and balls are widely available at *thrift shops* and *secondhand sporting goods stores*. You may want to point that fact out to the parents of your players in your initial contacts with them.
- *Baseball caps* for shielding eyes and avoiding sunburn are perfectly fine—and, in fact, helpful—for your young soccer players. You needn't worry about caps getting in the way of your players heading the ball because that skill is still in your players' future.

Your Equipment for Practices

Now that you know the equipment the players on your team will need for practices and games, it's time to look to your needs as coach.

By far the most important thing you need to "bring" to each practice is a *positive attitude*. Think Barney. Think kindergarten teacher. In other words, be sure to arrive at each practice with a smile on your face, ready to laugh and have fun with your players.

If you haven't worked with young children in groups before, the idea of coaching a bunch of energetic youngsters may be daunting to you. That's understandable. Even so, although it's natural to be a bit nervous about running your team's first practice, there's no need to dread it. Remember, your players just want to have fun—and they crave leadership. As long as you lead, you'll be followed by your players. The simplest way to lead your young players is to closely follow the practice sessions detailed in the last chapter of this book.

In addition to showing up for practices ready to have fun, the specific coaching equipment you'll need to bring with you includes the following items.

Raised Plastic Disc Cones

You'll use forty-nine of these inch-high, doughnut-shaped disc cones to mark grids for the activities you'll undertake during each practice. A number of soccer websites offer these disks in many colors. They're also available at specialty soccer stores and large sporting goods stores, though not yet widely available at department stores.

You'll use both traditional cones (left) and disc cones (right) during your team practices.

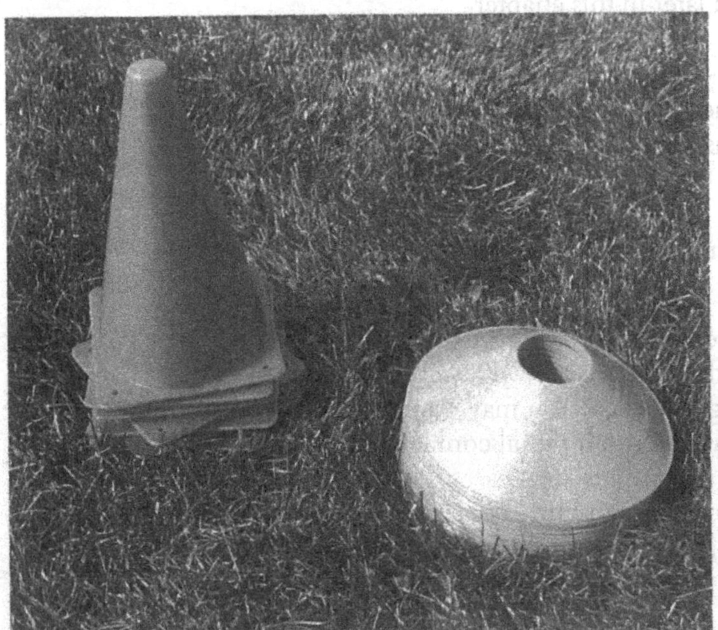

Cylindrical Plastic Cones

You'll use twenty of these widely available, traditional-style tall cones within the grids during the drills (though you'll use the term "games" with your players) that will form the heart of your practices.

Extra Balls

You'll need three or four extra balls to supply to the players whose parents invariably allow their children to show up without a ball.

Remember, at this age it's not the kids' fault if they come to practice unprepared. Displaying to your players any of the frustration you may feel about this lack of preparedness on the part of their parents will only turn your players off the game of soccer.

Over the years, we've made a habit of picking up used balls from thrift stores and garage sales. We plaster our names and phone numbers on the balls with black markers and give them out to our players without concern. If some of those used balls don't make their way back to us—as is inevitable—there's always next week's boffo multifamily yard sale at which we can pick up another ball or two.

Ball Pump

Some of your players will show up for practice with under-inflated balls. Such balls are difficult to dribble and control. It takes only a minute to pump up under-inflated balls until they're firm. You'll help your players significantly by taking a small amount of time before the start of practice to do so.

Clipboard

Your clipboard should hold a team roster and a photocopy of the correct practice session from the last chapter of this book. (Some coaches slip their rosters and practice schedules inside plastic sleeves before clipping them to their clipboards for protection from the elements.) You could also carry the roster and correct practice session folded in your pocket.

Use of the roster will help you memorize the names of your players, after which you'll no longer need it.

Watch

You'll need a watch to track length of drills and practices.

Mesh Bibs

Assuming you have more than six players on your team and will be dividing them into two squads to run through drills with a parent helper, you'll have an easier time keeping the squads separated if you divide them with bibs or reversed shirts at the beginning of each practice.

If your league requires goalkeepers, bring a mesh bib to your games for the goalkeeper to wear. At the 6-and-under level, there's scant risk of goalkeepers being accidentally kicked or trampled by attacking players. Still, having your goalkeeper wear a mesh bib and, in so doing, making your goalkeeper look different than the rest of the players on the field will further minimize that risk.

Mesh bibs are available at large sporting goods stores and at online and brick-and-mortar soccer stores, but at $7 or so each they're not cheap. As a less expensive alternative, consider buying like-colored T-shirts from a thrift shop for 50¢ or so each; then take scissors to them to convert them into bibs.

Full Water Bottle

This is for you.

We use our full-on involvement in each of our active practices as our workout for that day. Assuming you actively participate in your practices as well, you'll need water during and after practice as much as your players.

Water Jug and Small Paper Cups (optional)

This isn't essential given the short practices you'll hold with your young players—and, admittedly, it's a bit of a pain to bring in addition to everything else. However, cups of water can be very beneficial to players whose parents invariably will send their children to practice without their own bottles, especially on hot afternoons. Besides, keeping young children adequately hydrated is always a good thing.

Now for two pieces of equipment, often suggested for coaches of older players, that you *won't* need.

Whistle

Teachers don't use whistles in their classrooms. You won't need one as a coach.

See the following chapter, Behavioral Challenges of Young Players, for tips on gaining the attention of your players without a whistle and without raising your voice.

Collapsible Goals

The only drill in this book that requires goals is Drill 11: Steal the Bacon. Pairs of cones set a few feet apart work perfectly well as goals for the Steal the Bacon drill.

Your Equipment for Games

You won't need much equipment on game days. Just bring:

- A good attitude. As with practices, the most important thing for you to bring to games is a *positive, rah-rah attitude*. The cheerier you are with your players—slapping high fives with them, telling them how much they look like pro soccer players in their uniforms, offering words of encouragement one-on-one or to the entire team—the more your players will appreciate having you as their coach. Moreover, the more willing you are to laugh and be silly—to abandon adult conventionality and join your players in their happy-go-lucky world—the more fun your players will have.
- A *roster* folded in your pocket if you don't yet have the names of all your players memorized.
- Three or four *extra balls* to be kicked around the field a bit before the game by players who don't bring their own. Choose one of your well-

The cheerier you are with your players, the more they'll appreciate having you as their coach.

inflated #3 size balls or that of one of your players as the game ball if your opposing coach does not.

And that's all.

Here's what you won't need:

- As noted above, you won't need a *whistle*, even if you act as a referee. Whistles will be necessary for referees to halt and restart play when your players are older. For now, a slightly raised speaking voice is perfectly sufficient.
- Also, because games are for your players to run around and have fun while you remain on the sidelines as much as possible, you won't necessarily need a bottle of *water* for yourself.
- There's no need to bring any *cones* for setting up and running any official drills with your players to warm them up before their game, though you may do so if you wish. On cold or wet game days in particular, you may want to have players kick their balls around a grid you set up away from the playing field while they're waiting for their turn to play.

Game days are for your players. Leave your coaching equipment at home, come with a fun-loving attitude, and you'll have a great time during your team's games.

Choosing a Team Name

Q. Wait a minute. I'm about ready to take the field with my team, but we don't have a name yet. How should I take care of that?

A. Time was, coaches picked names for their teams and that was that.

These days, however, many coaches allow their players to choose the names of their teams. You'll please your young players no end if you do the same. In fact, young players love naming their teams so much that we recommend you allow your players to choose a new team name every season.

We've adopted a team-naming method from other coaches that works well. The method's two hallmarks are *fairness* and *assurance* that no players' feelings get hurt. Here's how the method works:

At the start of your first practice, tell your players they'll be selecting a team name at the end of practice and that they should be thinking of ideas for team names while they're practicing. At the end of practice, seat your players before you and ask those who have ideas for team names to raise their hands. If you're lucky, only two or three players will raise their hands right away. Before more players raise their hands, quickly have those two or three players stand and turn to face their teammates. If, as is more likely, all your players raise their hands, quickly select three players from among the upraised hands to stand and face the rest of their teammates.

Instruct each standing player to state her idea for the team name, and then have the standing players return to their seated positions. Give the team a moment to mull over the two or three ideas.

Now comes the important part: Have all your players lower their heads and cover their eyes with one hand. Then instruct them to vote for one, and only one, team name.

State each suggested team name and count the number of raised hands in favor of that idea. The name with the most votes wins. (In the case of a tie, feel free to go with the name you like best.)

Finally, have your players raise their heads and uncover their eyes. With great fanfare, announce the name of your team and lead your players in a loud cheer using their new name.

It's worth noting that by allowing 6-and-under players to pick team names, you'll generally end up with some fairly predictable choices such as the Lions, the Tigers, the Bears, and so on. However, you'll likely end up with some unusual choices as well. As far as we're concerned, the more unusual the name, the cuter and therefore the better. Two of our favorites, among the many 6-and-under teams we've coached over the years, have been the Toothless Warriors and the Fighting Rainbow Lions.

It's also worth noting that as your young players grow older, their name choices will grow wilder. At that point you may choose to do some vote rigging—an easy thing to do when your players' heads are bowed and their eyes covered. We shot down a vote by a team of 8-year-olds in favor of naming themselves Mad Cow Disease as being too insensitive, for example, but we loved another team's choice: the Savage Dung Beetles.

CHAPTER 6

Behavioral Challenges of Young Players

Quick Coaching Guide

You'll destroy your bond with your young players if you punish them for any perceived infractions you imagine them to have committed.

Use positive, time-tested responses to the behavioral challenges you're sure to face with various members of your team.

If you haven't noticed yet, children in the 4-to-6 age range are their own breed. In soccer-speak, they're known as "developmental players." In the language of this book, that means they're "little kids." Specifically, that means:

- Their *attention spans* are measured in nanoseconds—which is why, by using the practice sessions in this book, you'll keep them constantly on the go during practices.
- They're oriented to *"me, myself, and I"*—which is why the drills we recommend in this book are aimed at developing your players' individual skills through individual play activities.
- They're *constantly in motion*—and therefore will benefit greatly from the practice sessions in this book, which encourage them to move constantly.
- They're *easily bruised psychologically*—which is why you must always be positive with your players and work to be sure the parents of your players remain equally positive.
- They don't have the ability to pace themselves; they only know how to go *flat out*—which explains why the practices in this book are short and focused.

Discipline

Because young soccer players are different than older soccer players, they must be coached differently than older players, and they must be disciplined differently as well.

"There's no better way for you to destroy your bond with your young players than to punish them for any perceived infractions you imagine them to have committed. Your players are showing up to have fun playing the game of soccer, not to be victimized. If you turn the tables on them by punishing them, you'll damage their self-esteem, and you may well turn them off soccer and team sports for years, if not for life. Don't do it."

Most soccer coaching books for older players recommend the use of light punishment to keep players focused during practices, or demerits for losing various competitive drills to other team members. These forms of light punishment, sometimes called forfeits, may include running laps, doing a few push-ups, or singing silly songs or performing silly dances in front of teammates.

You should *never* use any of these forms of punishment with your 6-and-under players. Your players simply are not old enough to handle this type of discipline. No matter how lightly you attempt to punish them, they will not understand what you're trying to accomplish. They'll understand only that they're being punished, and that you're the one punishing them.

There's no better way for you to destroy your bond with your young players than to punish them for any perceived infractions you imagine them to have committed. Your players are showing up to have fun playing the game of soccer, not to be victimized. If you turn the tables on them by punishing them, you'll damage their self-esteem, and you may well turn them off soccer and team sports for years, if not for life. *Don't do it.*

How, then, to handle the many behavioral challenges your young players will present you with?

Below are the most common challenges you'll face, along with solutions:

The Nonlistener

The kid who just doesn't listen (which will be most, if not all, your players): Experts tell us 15 percent of all young children suffer from some form of attention-deficit/hyperactivity disorder. The rest, we assume, simply haven't learned how to pay attention yet.

Either way, holding the attention of your players and keeping them focused during practices will be your biggest challenge as a 6-and-under coach.

The key to a successful 6-and-under practice is to use the practice sessions in Chapter 10 of this book to keep your players moving. Simply stated, the way to handle young kids who don't listen well because they're young kids is to avoid requiring them to listen at all.

Over and over again, we have watched 6-and-under coaches sit their players down and try to explain a soccer concept to them. As we learned early on in our own young-player coaching careers, that idea just doesn't fly with the 6-and-under crowd.

It's true that sitting in a circle and listening to a teacher works, for a few minutes at a time anyway, in preschool, kindergarten, and first-grade settings. But youngsters on a soccer field are there to play. Your best bet is to let them.

Rather than lecture your players, get them doing the fun-based activities recommended for each of your practice sessions; then walk among them, demonstrating and helping them learn, on an individual basis, the techniques you want to teach them.

There still will be times you'll need to gain your players' attention—when it's time to shift them from one drill to another, for example. Various methods will work to grab their interest, including:

"Simply stated, the way to handle young kids who don't listen well because they're young kids is to avoid requiring them to listen at all."

- Counting backward from 10.
- Clapping rhythmically. Two long claps followed by three short ones is most common.
- Singing what you want them to do next.
- Using a silly voice to tell them what you want them to do—perhaps that of a clown or an old cowpoke.
- Using an accented voice—British perhaps, or French.

If you use a variety of the above ideas each practice, you'll have an easy time gaining your players' attention because you'll be playing to their natural curiosity. While they go about a drill, they'll be wondering just what method you're going to use the next time you need to gain their attention. When that time comes, they'll immediately pay attention to you just to satisfy their curiosity.

The Talker

The individual kid who just will not stop talking: Unless you're really lucky, you'll have one or two players on your team who are more rambunctious and have shorter attention spans than the other players on the team.

These players represent a more vexing problem than the natural restlessness of any group of young children in general. When one of your players continues to babble while you're trying to speak to the team, you can respond in any of several ways:

- Use the child's name as you talk. This often has the result of quieting the kid as he listens for when you'll use his name again.
- Lean over and speak directly to the talkative kid as you address the entire group. Again, your leaning toward the talker likely will silence him in mid-babble.
- Silently and nonchalantly separate the talker from the rest of the group and have him stand beside you, facing the team, as you complete your remarks.
- Ignore the offender. If you keep your remarks brief, as you should, you may well be able to complete what you have to say before the talkative player's nonstop commentary infects and distracts the rest of the team.

If none of the above works, and the talkative child proves a distinct detriment to the rest of the team's opportunity to play and learn soccer, you may need to sit the child down at the edge of the field for a couple of minutes. Generally, a minute or two spent watching from the sidelines as the rest of the team has fun will convince a talker to control himself a bit more in the future.

Finally, it's worth remembering that children with attention-deficit/hyperactivity disorder and borderline ADHD are members of our society, and accepting them as members of your team—disruptive though they may be at times—may well be part of your lot as a volunteer coach.

The Onlooker

The kid who just wants to sit on the sidelines and watch: Such children are common in the 6-and-under age bracket. Watching and studying something new before attempting it is a common learning tool employed by many young children. Such a response is fine. It's even laudatory. (Would that teenagers had as much common sense.)

You should welcome such players' desire to watch, include them as part of the team in every other way possible, and get on with teaching the players on the field.

The Space Cadet

The kid who spends her time on the field seemingly in outer space, either turning in circles, picking blades of grass and inspecting them intently, or staring up at the clouds: As with children reluctant to join in the activity on the field, allow such children as much space to be spacey as they need. Just make sure they're away from the action so they don't get trampled. They'll

Allow "space cadets" as much space as they need.

come around and get their heads into the game of soccer if and when they're good and ready. Nothing you can do will hasten the process. If anything, any attempts you make to force outer-space players to focus more on soccer will simply delay the coming-around process.

And if some of your players never come around? Well, is there really anything so wrong with that?

The Tackler

The kid who keeps tackling other players: Employ positive discipline by complimenting the player's tackling ability and lamenting the fact he isn't on a Pop Warner football team. Then endeavor to keep the tackler busy with the rest of the team.

Tacklers and their ilk—ticklers and wrestlers—tend to show up only when players are idle. Keep your kids moving, and the battle often will be won.

As with hard-core talkers, however, hard-core tacklers/ticklers/wrestlers may need for you to remove them from the action for a couple of minutes at a time. Seat them on the sidelines for a minute or two, watching their teammates play and have fun, and they'll generally return to the action less apt to create problems on the field.

Be forewarned, however: repeated sideline sessions may be necessary for repeat tacklers/ticklers/wrestlers. That's simply one of the realities of coaching young players.

If two of your players would rather wrestle with one another than participate in practices—a common occurrence—be sure to assign them to separate squads during your practice sessions.

The Crier

The kid who gets serial "ouchies" and runs crying to his parent every 5 minutes: Let him go. Don't try to call him back right away. Allow him to sit in his parent's lap as long as he wants. Make sure he feels welcome to return to practice or the game at any time, but don't push the issue. As long as you don't make him feel bad, he'll come around as he matures in the months ahead—at which point he may well prove to be the hardiest player on the team.

The Drill Hater

The kid who, for whatever reason, despises a particular practice drill and lets everybody around her know it: You can't please everybody. Sometimes that seems especially true of little kids.

If one of your players doesn't like a particular drill, don't make her participate in it. If a majority of your players turn against a particular drill, don't get your dander up. Simply choose another drill instead—preferably one that emphasizes the same skills.

Bad attitudes are contagious. If you've got a serial complainer on your hands, ask her to voice her complaints to you in private so her attitude doesn't infect the rest of the team.

The "All-Star"

The kid who is "better"—that is, more coordinated—than everyone else on the team: Don't discourage him. But don't give him preferential treatment either, especially in terms of giving him additional playing time during games. If you do, the rest of the team will grow accustomed to having him control everything on the field for them.

Remember: Eventually soccer will become a true team sport for your players. Your team and all its players will be harmed irreparably—and will lose regularly in the years ahead, when one or two players can no longer control a game—if you give your more coordinated players preferential treatment during these early years of play.

"Eventually soccer will become a true team sport for your players. Your team and all its players will be harmed irreparably—and will lose regularly in the years ahead, when one or two players can no longer control a game—if you give your more coordinated players preferential treatment during these early years of play."

The Ambulance Watcher

The kid who stops in the middle of an important drill to watch a fire truck or ambulance pass by: At the 6-and-under age level, that includes just about every player.

Simply call a time-out, watch along with your players until the vehicle is out of sight, then get back to practice.

It's worth noting that though the behavioral challenges outlined in this chapter may seem intimidating, many will never be an issue for you, and most—if not all—that do arise will fade away as the season progresses and you and your players settle into your practice and game-day routines.

Game Day

Quick Coaching Guide

Enjoy your young team's games for all they're worth. Savor them. They'll be over and gone in an instant.

Six-and-under practices are for learning while having fun; 6-and-under games are purely for fun.

Winning and losing should in no way be a part of what your team's games are about.

Always offer to provide the referee for your team's games; then consider carefully who to ask. A good referee can go a long way toward making your young players' first experiences with competitive game play positive and uplifting.

It's finally time for your first game. Your players are excited. You are, too—plus, perhaps, a little apprehensive. That's only natural. Remember, however, that this is what it's all about: Youngsters playing the game of soccer. And remember, too, that you're about to have the time of your life.

Many times we've heard parents of older players talk about how much they miss the first years their children played soccer, when the games were a big happy mess and nobody knew the score and the players were just as happy dog-piling atop one another or picking dandelions or stopping to watch a loud motorcycle drive by as they were actually playing their games. To which we say, "Hear, hear."

Gone in an Instant

The most important thing you should know about the official games your team will play during these first couple of years of soccer is that the games will be over and gone in an instant. Your team members will be youth soccer players rather than little-kid soccer players faster than you can even think about it. Magically, it will seem, their games will have taken on a semblance of real soccer.

Few goals will be scored. Passes will be attempted and some completed. Goalkeepers will actually stop shots.

More's the pity.

Our advice to you as coach? Enjoy your young team's games for all they're worth. Savor them. Smile with your team's parents at the antics of your pint-sized players on the field.

Step back from your role as coach as much as possible during your team's games. Allow yourself to be a member of the audience, to enjoy the wonderful spectacle of your players chasing a confoundingly elusive ball around the field in their matching shirts and too-big cleats and floppy shin guards.

Most important, relax.

Repeat after us: Six-and-under soccer games are virtually meaningless when it comes to learning the game of soccer.

Let's try that again: Six-and-under soccer games are *virtually meaningless*.

"Six-and-under soccer games are virtually meaningless when it comes to learning the game of soccer."

The greatest thing about your team's official games is that they provide your players with the opportunity to put on their uniforms, run around in front of their cheering parents, and—probably most important—have a treat with their teammates afterward. Your team's games enable you, your players, and their parents to have a whole bunch of fun—and they justify the weekly practices during which your players will learn most, if not all, the soccer they'll pick up throughout the season.

Little Learning

Think again about any few minutes of professional soccer you've caught on television. The camera was focused on the ball, the player handling the ball, and the defensive player trying to steal the ball away. But what about the other twenty players on the field? They were on the move, surely, working to get into position to receive or deny a pass or block a goal. But they weren't touching or moving the ball.

Logic indicates, and studies prove, that the average soccer player controls the ball for only 2 minutes during any game. That's 2 *minutes*. And that's in a game with older kids or adults.

Six-and-under games are shorter than older-kid games. Moreover, during any 6-and-under game, one or two players from each team invariably control the ball the vast majority of the game (not because they're necessarily better soccer players, but because their coordination skills are a few months ahead of those of the other players on the field).

Every now and then during a 6-and-under game, the more coordinated players don't manage to maintain control of the ball. That's generally when the ball disappears amid a swarm of all the rest of the players from both teams. After a few seconds of flailing kicks, the ball suddenly pops free, and once again, one of the more coordinated players takes off dribbling it up the field—perhaps in the correct direction, perhaps not—with the rest of the players from both teams in pursuit.

Not a lot of learning occurs during 6-and-under games, that's for sure. But, oh, what wonderful things they are to watch—which is exactly what you, as coach, should feel free to do.

Winning and Losing

As busy and focused as you'll be as a coach during the vigorous practices you'll hold for your young players, you can and should be just as relaxed during your team's games.

The key to being relaxed is to remember that winning and losing should in no way be a part of what your team's games are about.

Indeed, it's worth your knowing that 6-and-under games are quite easy to "win"—though you're the one who will be the loser in the process. All you have to do is drop a player back to play defense. That is, don't allow one member of your team to play soccer. Your defensive player will slow or shut down most of the other team's offensive breakaways, and your team likely will go on to "win."

But at what expense?

You'll have eliminated the opportunity for one of your players to do what all your players want to do—run up and down the field trying to kick the ball while their parents watch.

Plus, you'll very quickly force the other coaches in your age group to follow suit. At that point, not only will you have spoiled every game for one of your players, you'll have spoiled all the games for one player from every other team as well. Not exactly something to be proud of. And certainly not something worth "winning" 6-and-under soccer games for.

Instead, let your players play soccer on game days. If other coaches hit upon the idea of pulling their players out of the action and dropping them back on defense, don't follow suit. So what if that means your team doesn't score as many goals as the other team? That fact has nothing to do with 6-and-under soccer. Besides, your players will spend a whole bunch of time in the future working at and eventually mastering position play. Six-and-under soccer is not the time for it.

Six-and-under soccer coaches who encourage every one of their team members to play offensive, go-for-the-ball soccer every minute of every game are true winners. All young-player coaches—including you—should strive to be that type of coach.

"Six-and-under soccer coaches who encourage every one of their team members to play offensive, go-for-the-ball soccer every minute of every game are true winners. All young-player coaches—including you—should strive to be that type of coach."

A Word or Two Concerning Position Play

Many coaches of young players quickly move beyond simply dropping a player back to play defense. They begin teaching their young team members to play positions very early in their soccer careers.

When should you begin thinking about position play for your players? Consider the following:

A successful college coach we know recruited a player who had immigrated to the United States from Brazil before his senior year of high school and so had played only a single season of 11-on-11, position-style American soccer. Prior to that, the young Brazilian played a form of soccer in Brazil called *futsal* that involves the use of a small ball on a small field, a handful of players, and little in the way of position play.

In other words, the Brazilian spent all his time as a youth playing a form of soccer that required him to use all the basic skills of soccer all the time—rather than spending great wads of time standing in a remote position on a huge field watching other members of his team play soccer.

The result?

The player led his U.S. college team—one of the top teams for its size in the country—in goals and assists his freshman year.

"His skills were so refined that he could step right in and take command of the team," the coach said of his Brazilian player. "Teaching him to play a position was simple compared to that."

The lesson for you as a 6-and-under coach?

Focus on teaching your players basic ball-control skills as detailed in the following chapter. Don't worry about winning and losing, and don't be tempted to require your players to play specific positions during games anytime soon.

Only when your players have repeated basic ball-control skills thousands of times will they attain mastery of those skills, and only after they've mastered those basic skills will they truly be ready for position-play soccer.

Don't rush things. Have fun running through the basic skills and drills with your players, as detailed in this book, for as long as possible. (In fact, the competitive drills in this book are great for players all the way through high school.)

Concentrate on teaching your young players basic skills during your fun-filled practices, enjoy the swarm style of soccer for the messy spectacle it is, and avoid introducing your players to position play until you absolutely have to. Your players will be the direct beneficiaries of such an approach.

Game-Day Responsibilities

As coach you have only a handful of game-day jobs:

Run the Warm-up

There's not much to this responsibility. Just make sure your players loosen up a bit by kicking balls into a goal or by playing Switch (see Drill 4, pages 96–97) for a few minutes before the start of the game.

Older players generally are expected to arrive 30 to 45 minutes before the start of their games, but there's no need for you to expect that of your young players and their parents. If you want parents of your players to have their kids at the field 10 or 15 minutes before games so that you can have fun warming up with your players and they with you, feel free to ask. If you'd rather have everyone simply show up at game time, that's fine, too. Remember: practices are for learning, games are for fun.

Hold a Team Cheer

Before the start of each game, gather your team around you, hands extended inward, and shout out together whatever team cheer you like—the word "go" followed by your team name works well, as do any and all more complicated offerings you and your players may cook up together. The important thing is to perform some sort of cheer to honor and recognize your players' new and exciting roles as members of a team.

Face Your Players in the Right Direction

Trot onto the field and position your players on their correct half of the field, facing the goal they're aiming for, at the start of each quarter and after goals are scored; then return to the sidelines.

Equalize Playing Time

Ensure that all players who want it are afforded equal playing time. The parents of your players may not have stopwatches in their hands, but they'll have them in their heads, and they'll know if you've shortchanged little Emily.

Ensure That Your Least Coordinated Players Get Equal Time on the Field

It's particularly important to ensure that your least coordinated players get equal playing time at this age. Though it doesn't appear so when one or two players control the game—as happens during every 6-and-under contest—soccer is a true team sport. Like all sports teams, your soccer team will only be as strong as its weakest player in the years to come. If you sideline your weakest players now in order to score more goals than other teams in games that don't mean a thing to your players, you'll only be curtailing the success of your players in later years, when winning and losing will become matters of immense importance to them.

Moreover, in many cases the weakest players at the 6-and-under level go on to become the strongest players on their teams when they mature—as long as they're given the opportunity to play and improve. Often, weak players grow determined to master the sport and are willing to spend the hours away from the field working on juggling and other ball-control skills that make them stronger players. Conversely, top 6-and-under players are as likely to coast on their glory and fade into mediocrity over time as they are to remain the stars of their teams for the long haul.

Besides, 6-and-under soccer is not about who's a better or worse player. On game day especially, but throughout the season as well, 6-and-under soccer is about nothing more—and nothing less—than having fun.

Every single one of your players deserves an equal opportunity to have fun on the field. Doing all you can to assure that all your players are afforded that opportunity is the only really crucial job you have as coach on game day.

Accommodate Reluctant Players

If a kid doesn't want to join in the melee on game day, don't make her do so. Let her parents know that they needn't urge their daughter to play either.

Kids know their likes and dislikes. They know when they're comfortable trying something new and when they're not. There's no need to force them to do something they don't want to do.

We've had several kids refuse to play a single minute of soccer during practices and games their entire first season. For the most part those kids never missed a practice or game, however. They were content to sit on the sidelines and vicariously soak up the action. In all those cases, by the next season those formerly reluctant players were among the most enthusiastic players on the field, during practices and games alike.

If your subs would rather sit in their parents' laps than near you on the sidelines, that's fine.

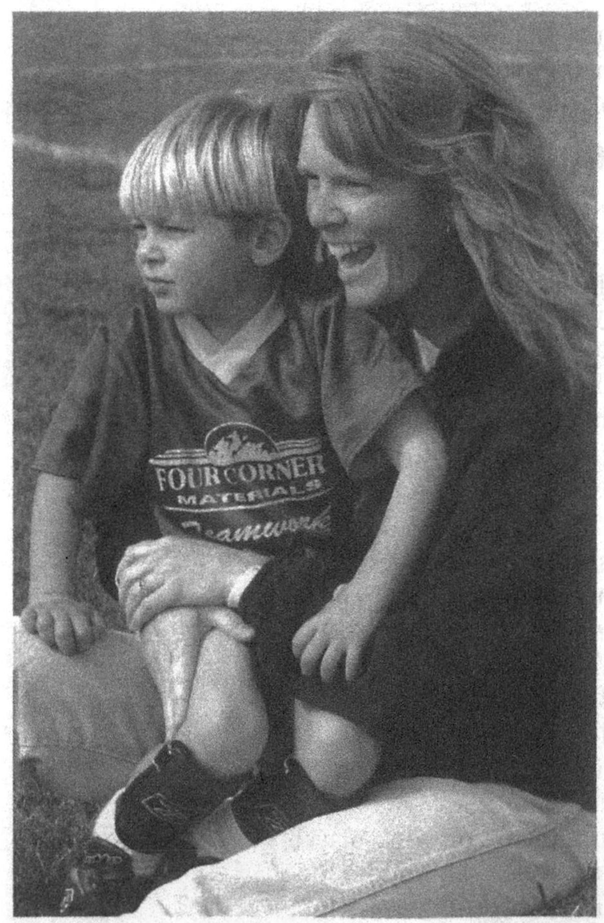

What if we'd forced those reluctant children to take the field and play? We likely would have chased them away from the game for good.

Likewise, in the unlikely event that any of your players are reluctant to participate in practices but want to play during your team's games, let them. Your job as coach is to encourage your young players to play soccer whenever they're comfortable doing so.

Keep Your Subs as Close to You as Possible on the Sidelines

To the extent possible, keep your subs sitting near you along the sidelines. That way, when a player on the field grows tired and sluggish or gets an "ouchie," you can send in a fresh player right away. If, however, your subs would rather sit in their parents' laps or if they otherwise wander away, that's fine. And if, as a result, your team ends up playing shorthanded for a minute or two when one player comes out and it takes you a while to round up a sub, so be it. This isn't the World Cup.

We once noticed, while standing on the sidelines watching one of our teams play a game, that all three subs from our team had wandered off behind the spectators, where they were engaged in a furious, all-on-all wrestling match.

"Hey!" one of us barked at them in a gruff voice. They stopped wrestling and looked up. "You're acting like a bunch of kindergartners over there!"

They eyed one another in guilty silence for a moment. Then their eyes brightened in dawning recognition.

"But we *are* kindergartners!" the bravest of the three piped up.

To which came the reply: "That's right. So keep doing what you're doing. We'll call for you when it's your turn to play."

Don't Chase the Action All Over the Field

Many 6-and-under coaches chase the action around the field, barking orders at their players while their teams are trying to play. Except for positioning your players on the correct half of the field at the start of quarters or after a goal is scored, however, there's no need for you to be on the field.

Game time is your players' opportunity to run around on the field, not yours. It's their chance to show off their matching jerseys and brand-new cleats. It's their chance to shine. Your running around the field yelling directions at your players to kick the ball at the correct goal—or, worse, to actually give up the ball by passing it to one of their teammates—only diminishes their four short quarters of glory.

Still, if you want to join your team on the field during the game, that's your privilege as coach (unless your league forbids it). You'll certainly get a closer view of the game that way. Just don't kid yourself into thinking you'll be teaching your players anything. Whatever you tell your young players will be wasted breath; they'll be too busy applying what they've learned from you in practice to listen to you during games. Instead, your best bet is to let your kids play their unique brand of little-kid soccer while you enjoy every fleeting second of it from the sidelines.

Don't Scream and Yell Directions at Your Players

If you want to offer words of encouragement and praise to individual players as they pass by you on the sidelines during a game, by all means do so. But hollering clear across the field to get a kid to move closer to the goal or attempt a pass or take a shot will only make you look silly.

This is 6-and-under soccer. The intricacies of game play—positioning, passing, shooting—will come soon enough. Be thankful you don't have to worry about all that right now.

Coordinated Player Substitutions

Within the first game or two of your first season, you and everyone else will easily recognize the more coordinated, more advanced players on each team.

In light of this recognition, you may want to confer with your opposing coach before each game to coordinate your teams' substitutions so as to ensure that the strong players from both teams are on and off the field at roughly the same time during the game.

Such teamwork between you and other coaches will help make all your games more even and, therefore, more competitive. Far more important, when you and your opposing coaches remove your teams' more coordinated players from the field at the same time, you'll effectively provide your teams' less coordinated players a much greater opportunity to actually kick the ball once or twice while their parents proudly look on.

The 30-Second Goalkeeping Tutorial

If your league calls for you to use goalkeepers for your 6-and-under games, you may want to suggest to your opposing coaches, on a game-by-game basis, the idea of not using them. Each time an opposing coach agrees with you and you don't have to use goalkeepers, your players and those of the other team will benefit.

Often enough, your opposing coach will insist on using goalkeepers because "that's the way it's always been done" or "that's what the rules say." When that happens, you'll have an opportunity to teach a little soccer on game day.

We don't recommend that you teach goalkeeping to your players during your practices. Teaching goalkeeping during 6-and-under practices takes too much time away from encouraging players to move the ball with their feet; practice time is simply too limited to waste any of it on goalkeeping. Besides, teaching goalkeeping—that is, grabbing the ball with the hands—is directly opposite the primary idea you're trying to teach your young players, which is that they should touch the ball with their feet, and never with their hands.

Moreover, goalkeeping is a solitary occupation best taught to one player at a time while everyone else stands around and grows restive—not a good idea with the 6-and-under crowd. Instead, if and when you must have goalkeepers in games, we suggest you use a different player in goal each quarter, then give a quick, 30-second tutorial on goalkeeping to each goalkeeper before the start of the quarter, working your way through the entire team as the season progresses, and repeating the tutorial with individual players as necessary.

The 30-second tutorial consists of instructing the goalkeeper to:

1. Find her correct position by standing midway between the two goalposts on the line between the posts, then taking one giant step forward.
2. Remain one giant step's distance in front of the goal line.
3. Move back and forth between the goalposts with the movement of the ball from one side of the field to the other so as to remain between the ball and the mouth of the goal.

4. Have fun pretending to be an octopus by pouncing on the ball with her arms and entire body whenever the ball comes within the painted goal box surrounding the goal. (Over the years, we've found that the octopus analogy works well to help 6-and-under players make the switch from playing soccer with their feet to guarding the goal with their hands.)
5. Instantly jump up after pouncing on the ball, run with it to the nearest corner of the goal box, and quickly heave it as far down that side of the field as possible.
6. Immediately return to her position in front of the goal, one giant step in front of the goal mouth.

As part of the 30-second tutorial, run your goalkeeper through the process three or four times by gently rolling a ball toward her on the ground. During the dry runs, emphasize that she should 1) hold her location in front of the goal, 2) pounce on the ball only when it comes into the goal box, 3) quickly throw it back into play from the nearest corner of the goal box, and 4) run back to her position in front the goal right away, ready for the next shot to come her way.

Postgame Handshake and Cheer

Immediately following each game, line your players up to walk past and shake hands with the members of the other team. Be sure you shake hands with and thank the opposing coach, no matter how over-the-top she may have been on the competitiveness scale.

If spectators form an "arc of triumph" with their outstretched arms, enjoy watching your players run through it a few times while the spectators cheer them on.

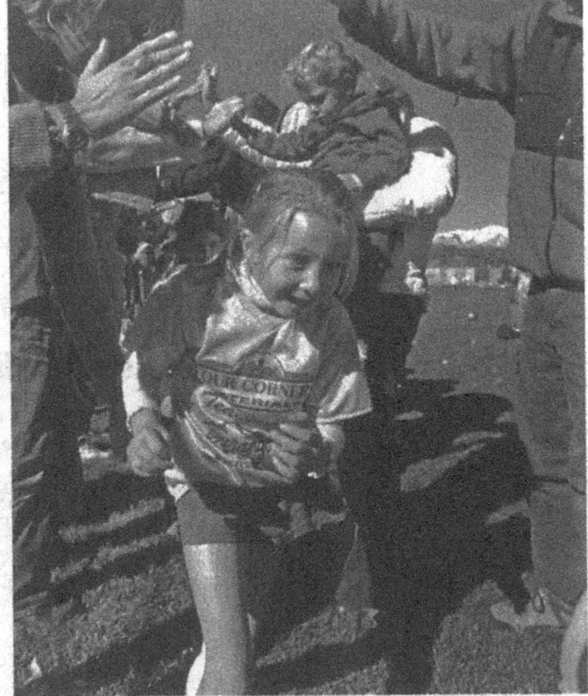

If spectators form an "arc of triumph" with their outstretched arms, enjoy watching your team run through it a few times as the spectators cheer them on. Then gather your team around you for a quick debriefing.

First, have your team members gather in a circle, hands extended inward, to offer up a shouted cheer to the other team—"Good game, Colts!"

Next, tell your players how well they played and how proud you are of them. Then find something to compliment about the play of every member of your team. After each of your compliments, have the team clap and cheer for that particular player.

Finally, offer up a few more words of praise to all your players as a team before releasing them to the parent providing the end-of-game treat.

Refereeing

One of the unavoidable evils of 6-and-under soccer games is the need for someone to act as a supervisor during games. There's no need for a referee per se—that is, someone calling fouls and awarding penalty kicks. Still, the term "referee" is used for whoever supervises 6-and-under games.

There are several things to consider regarding the important issue of refereeing.

Decide Whether to Take On the Task Yourself

The best place for you to be during games is on the sidelines. There you can best enjoy watching the game with your players' parents. In addition, you can make substitutions as necessary, and you can visit with your off-the-field players, explaining what's happening on the field and what they can do to improve their play and thus have more fun when it's their turn to take the field.

Unfortunately, however, the simple fact is that control-freak referees often ruin 6-and-under soccer games. Far better that you should leave your subs under the watchful eye of one of your team's parents and referee your games yourself than let the game be ruined by someone else—provided you're dedicated to being a good referee.

Know Good Refs from Bad

A good 6-and-under game official is someone who understands that a full-on referee is not needed at this age level. All that's really necessary is for someone to oversee the game for the sake of safety. Rough or inappropriate play—tripping, elbowing, shoving—need simply be explained to the offending player, preferably while the game continues. In worst-case scenarios, a good referee should ask a coach to provide a substitution for an overly aggressive player.

The referee also needs to award kick-ins—or throw-ins, if your league's rules call for them and your opposing coach insists on them (see pages 23–24).

A good referee remains in the background as much as possible and just lets the kids play.

The referee must help the players with those kick-ins and help teams get lined up and facing the correct direction at the beginnings of quarters and after goals are scored.

A good referee keeps the game moving. Such a referee recognizes that a whole bunch of kids and parents have gone to the trouble of gathering for a 32-minute soccer game, and they deserve to play and watch as much soccer as possible during that short time. A good referee therefore encourages players to run, not walk, after the ball when it's kicked out-of-bounds, and then directs players to kick the ball back into play quickly. Overall, a good referee avoids stopping the game except for one reason—when a player's safety is at stake.

In contrast, a poor referee destroys the flow and fun of the game by stopping it repeatedly to, for example, lecture a player whose elbows may be swinging a bit wide when he runs, or to make players repeat throw-ins or kick-ins he views as having been performed improperly. A poor referee doesn't understand this simple admonition: Just let the kids play.

Be Proactive in Choosing a Referee

Always offer to provide the referee for your team's games. Then consider carefully who to ask. Most of all, you want to ask a spectator who is easygoing, who gets along well with children, who is patient and not quick to anger. Whether the spectator knows anything about soccer doesn't matter a bit.

You'll also want a referee who understands that quick games equal fun games, and who hustles accordingly.

If such a potential ref doesn't exist from among your players' parents and other spectators, consider taking on the role of referee yourself before turning the responsibility of choosing a ref over to the other team.

Say No to Two Refs

Some leagues suggest having two referees on the field during 6-and-under games, one from each team. Our take: One is too many, but necessary. Two is ridiculous—and harmful.

The whole point of little-kid soccer games is to let the kids run around and have fun with as little adult interference as possible. The addition of two referees invariably ruins the flow, feel, and fun of little-kid games.

No Whistles

Six-and-under game refs need the capacity to 1) get the ball back in play quickly when it goes out-of-bounds or after a goal is scored, and 2) step in and stop play momentarily when a player is injured, or falls and is endangered by a swarm of kids trying to kick the ball near him. Both tasks are easily accomplished without use of a whistle.

Positive Encouragement

If you can find a referee who trades high fives with kids from both teams when they score goals and who doles out praise and compliments to members of both teams throughout the game, so much the better. Such refs are gems who go a long way toward making your young players' first experiences with competitive game play positive and uplifting.

Live with the Referee You Get—Make Corrections Next Time

If the ref comes from the other team and doesn't display the positive attributes you'd like to see, there isn't a lot you can do about it at the time. Do, however, file away the memory of that game. The next time you play that team, kindly insist to the opposing coach that it's now your turn to choose the referee, then use your hand-picked ref—or take on the task yourself if necessary—to assure that, this time around, the game is refereed in a loose and positive manner that benefits your players and those of the other team.

Keeping Time

The referee on the field should keep time. Encourage the referee to use leeway in doing so. That is, be sure the referee halts play at the end of quarters or the game only when the ball goes out of play rather than halting play right to the second—when a youngster may well be dribbling the ball full tilt down the field with the chance to score what may prove to be the only goal of his entire youth soccer career.

Who Won?

Q. Many times, my players run up to me at the end of a game and ask with breathless anticipation whether we won or lost. This happens even if the other team scored a dozen goals to our one or two. How should I respond?

A. Tell them no official score was kept. Then go on to tell them they're all winners as far as you're concerned.

The fact that they're running up to you excitedly at the end of the game proves they are indeed winners, because winning soccer at the 6-and-under level is all about having fun. As long as your players have had fun on the field, they've won. The final score doesn't matter at all and should in no way be used to determine whether the players on your team won their game.

If your players insist on hearing from you which team scored more goals, don't lie to them. Tell them you think the other team may have scored more. Then go on to tell your players the truth—that at their age the final score doesn't determine which team "wins" or "loses" games. Rather, the idea at their age is for both teams to win every game by having lots of fun playing good competitive soccer with one another.

CHAPTER 8

Basic Ball-Control Skills and the Red Light/ Green Light Drill

Quick Coaching Guide

Effective ball control can be broken down into basic skills such as dribbling with the inside of the foot, dribbling with speed, cutting, pulling, receiving, and juggling.

Use the Red Light/Green Light drill to teach basic ball-control skills to your young players.

Never criticize your players' efforts. Rather than correct what your players are doing wrong, demonstrate to them how to do each skill, then praise whatever part of each skill they perform correctly when they try it.

It's time to get to the heart of what you'll be doing as a coach: having fun teaching basic ball-control skills to your young players.

You already know the game of soccer is based on ball movement and control. But how to teach your young players to move and control the ball effectively?

Effective ball movement and control can be broken down into basic skills. By teaching those skills, you'll teach your players to move and control the ball effectively on the soccer field—the key to becoming solid, game-loving soccer players in the years ahead.

Over time, and through our work with other coaches, we've developed a simple and straightforward method for teaching young players basic ball-control skills. That method involves the repeated use of a single fun drill, or game, for a few minutes at the beginning of each practice session.

The drill you'll use to introduce basic ball-control skills to your players over the course of your first six practice sessions is Red Light/ Green Light, a game most of your players likely already will know. If not, it's one they will pick up quickly—and it's one they're guaranteed to enjoy playing.

Before each practice, you'll lay out your players' "driving lanes" for the drill. (See diagram on page 67.) Then you'll begin each of your practices by running the drill with up to six of your players at a time. Each player needs to bring a #3 size soccer ball to every practice to use in this and the other drills.

If—as is most likely—you have between seven and twelve players on your team, you'll need to set up a rectangular drill grid, as noted in the following chapter, separate from your Red Light/Green Light driving-lanes grid. You'll then have your parent helper run a fun drill, or game, with half your players in the rectangular grid while you teach ball-control skills to the other half of your team by running Red Light/Green Light in the driving-lanes grid.

Green light! (1)

Red light! (2)

Why Red Light/Green Light?

Red Light/Green Light is a terrific drill for teaching ball-control skills to young players for a number of reasons:

1. Your young players will *love the idea* of "driving" down the "lanes" of the Red Light/Green Light grid (see page 67) while touching and moving the ball with their feet. Because Red Light/Green Light is fun, your players will enjoy starting every practice with it. Indeed, the more you play up the idea of your players as "drivers" (long-haul truckers, perhaps, or race-car drivers, or drivers of stagecoaches) the more they'll enjoy the drill, which they'll see as a game.
2. The *stop-and-go, do-this-and-do-that aspect* of Red Light/Green Light provides a perfect platform for teaching basic ball-control skills to 6-and-under players, who are too young to learn by listening to lectures. As coach, you'll control the drill by shouting out "traffic signals." Your players will be so involved in listening for your next "signal" that they'll perform the basic ball-control skills within the framework of the drill almost unthinkingly.
3. Red Light/Green Light *separates your players* into their own "driving lanes," enabling them to learn, practice, and develop basic ball-control skills on their own and at their own pace rather than in a confusing mass.

As a result, your players will pick up each new skill as you introduce it to them, and their overall soccer abilities will increase rapidly.

4. Red Light/Green Light enables you to *add* a new skill each week, *build* each skill one upon another, and *reinforce* the skills you've already taught your players.

Mastering Several Basic Skills through One Drill

You'll add a new "traffic signal," or ball-control skill, each time you run Red Light/Green Light. Then, as you run the drill, you'll call out the new signal as well as all the previous signals your players have learned to that point. As a result, your players quickly will learn the basic ball-control skills you introduce to them. They'll then begin to perform these skills during their games and other practice-session drills.

You'll use Red Light/Green Light to teach your young players six basic ball-control skills over the course of your first six practice sessions. There's no magic in the six particular skills you'll introduce to your players. Rather, the magic is in the overall concept of using Red Light/Green Light to introduce ball-control skills to your players.

The six skills we recommend here are simply half a dozen that happen to work well within the structure of the Red Light/Green Light drill. In addition, the six particular skills work well with the 6-and-under crowd—they're age-appropriate.

Some might well take issue with the six skills we suggest. (For your part, you might well want to try introducing other ball-control skills to your players within the Red Light/Green Light framework.) The six skills we include in this chapter are simply those that we have found, over the years, to work most effectively with Red Light/Green Light to best teach young soccer players how to move and control the ball with their feet.

Indeed, some might take issue with the entire concept of using Red Light/Green Light to introduce basic ball-control skills to 6-and-under players—or to introducing ball-control skills to 6-and-under players at all. Our response? Six-and-under soccer players are fully capable of beginning the process that will lead, eventually, to their mastering the ability to control the ball, and Red Light/Green Light provides a tremendous platform for doing so. There are countless ways to introduce the game of soccer to youngsters. What we present in this book is simply the method we've found to work best, based on years of research, trial and error, and refinement.

After your first six practices, you'll continue to use Red Light/Green Light in subsequent sessions and seasons to enable your players to refine their ball-control abilities.

Let's look first at how to run the Red Light/Green Light drill. Then we'll look at how to teach basic ball-control skills while you play Red Light/Green Light with your team.

Drill 1: Red Light/Green Light

Goal: Introducing basic ball-control skills.
Suggested Story Line: Truck driving (specifics noted below with each skill).
Setup: Driving-lanes grid (49 disc cones).

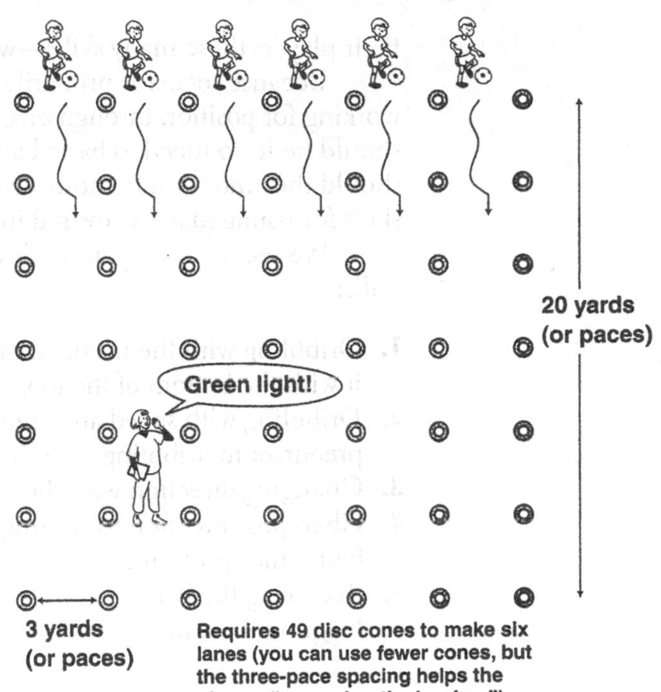
Green light!
20 yards
(or paces)
3 yards
(or paces)
Requires 49 disc cones to make six lanes (you can use fewer cones, but the three-pace spacing helps the players "remember the borders")

Red Light/Green Light

Getting Started

One of the most difficult aspects of Red Light/Green Light is getting your young players to line up in their individual driving lanes. Use the *Easter egg trick* to get this drill started quickly and easily by having your players put their heads down and close their eyes. Tell them the soccer bunny will hide their soccer balls, and that when they open their eyes, they are to find their balls as quickly as possible and stand with one foot on the ball. Quickly "hide" each player's ball at the start of a driving lane and call for your players to find their balls.

Your players will scatter to their soccer balls and stand, waiting expectantly. Don't hesitate. Immediately launch into the story line of your choosing or into the truck driver story line suggested for each new skill below. After telling your players your two- or three-sentence story, tell them *what* you want them to do. For your first practice, for example, tell them to "drive" their trucks with their soccer-ball cargo down their driving lanes when you call out "green light," and to stop with the bottoms of their feet on their cargo when they come to a "red light."

How to Run the Drill

Quickly send your players off by shouting out the "Green light!" traffic signal, and then follow up that signal with "Red light!" (and the other five signals in subsequent practices). While your players "drive" their soccer balls up and down their individual driving lanes in response to your traffic signals, walk among them offering embellishments to your story line, lots of praise, and only one suggestion for improvement per player per Red Light/Green Light session.

Basic Ball-Control Skills

Every soccer coaching book available today outlines advanced soccer skills such as goalkeeping, heading, defensive skills, sideline throw-ins, corner kicks, and position play. Most coaches of very young players thus try to teach their players these many skills—with harm and confusion the primary result.

Because soccer is primarily a game of touching and passing the ball, of working for position through crisp controlled ball movement, young players should be introduced to basic ball-control concepts first. Only after that should they move on to more advanced skills (including the four additional skills for young players covered in the following chapter).

We recommend you teach your players the following basic ball-control skills:

1. Dribbling with the inside of the foot and stopping the ball by stepping on it with the bottom of the foot
2. Dribbling with speed and "pushing" the ball with the instep as a precursor to dribbling with the outside of the foot
3. Changing direction with the inside of the foot, or "cutting" the ball
4. Changing direction by pulling the ball backward with the bottom of the foot—the "pull turn"
5. Receiving the ball
6. Juggling the ball

Skills 1 and 2 involve moving the ball, skills 3 and 4 involve changing the direction of the ball, and skills 5 and 6 involve controlling a moving ball.

Here are the seven commands, or "traffic signals," you'll use:

1. Green light!
2. Red light!
3. Hit the highway!
4. Roundabout!
5. U-turn!
6. Out of the sky!
7. Traffic jam!

A few points worth noting before we look at teaching each specific ball-control skill:

- You'll have the opportunity to introduce your players to *four additional skills* as part of four other drills you'll play with them during your practice sessions. The additional skills—shooting, passing, receiving, and shielding the ball—are detailed in the following chapter.
- One advanced skill in particular you absolutely *should not* teach your players is *heading the ball.* No studies prove any real danger from older players heading the ball correctly as part of playing advanced soccer. Still, everyone agrees young players' growing brains don't need the repeated blows that come from heading the ball.

  Though heading is far in your players' future, they'll try (and generally fail) to head the ball every now and then. There's no need for you to discourage those rare attempts at heading—except, if you wish, to minimize the risk of "nose balls" and resultant tears.

- In the remainder of this chapter we provide a great deal of commentary about each basic ball-control skill. *That commentary is for you,* the coach, not your players. Your job is to get your young players performing ball-control skills and then to work with them individually to get them performing those skills correctly. Reciting to your players any of the extensive coaching commentary we provide on each skill will only confuse them.
- When you set out to introduce each new ball-control skill to your players, your goal should be to *get them started doing the skill as quickly as possible.* Don't lecture your players. Instead, arrange them in their Red Light/Green Light lanes with their balls at their feet, briefly tell them *what* you want them to do—but not *how* you want them to do it—then have them get started doing it.

  To actually teach the skill, move among your players and show them the correct technique for that particular skill on an individual, one-on-one basis. Over the course of a few minutes, work your way through several of your players while you're calling out "traffic signals" and your players are performing the drill.

  (You won't, in fact, be teaching the skill one-on-one because players in neighboring lanes will stop to listen to what you're saying to one of your players and then will apply what you've said to their own efforts. Still, you won't be lecturing to the group as a whole either—which means you'll avoid the problems that inevitably arise when trying to lecture to a group of fidgety youngsters.)
- From your second practice on, remember to shout out Red Light/Green Light "traffic signals" directing your players to perform all the ball-control skills you've introduced so far, not just the skill you're introducing that day. From your seventh practice on, we suggest you shout out traffic signals for the ball-control skills you've introduced to them to that point without adding any more skills—or complexity—to the Red Light/Green Light drill.
- Most soccer players are right-footed. However, as soon as you've introduced a skill to your players and they've begun to master it, you should encourage them to perform the skill with *either foot.* It's never too early to explain to your players that talented soccer players use both feet with equal ability, and to suggest to your players that they, too, should use both feet as much as possible to move, control, and change direction of the ball.
- As you walk among your players describing the correct technique they should use to perform each ball-control skill, be sure you *don't turn negative.* Remember, you're the one expecting them to do something they've never done before without the benefit of being told how to do it. They *should* perform the skill incorrectly until you work with them. Rather than point out that fact to them, it's up to you to show and tell your play-

Exude Positivity

It's commonly accepted in coaching circles that when it comes to teaching very young players any sport, at least ten positive coaching comments are required to offset any one negative comment.

It's absolutely critical for you, as a coach of young soccer players, to always remember that your young players' self-esteem is just developing. In recognition of that fact, it's up to you to keep *all* your interactions with your players positive and upbeat.

When it comes to teaching your players basic ball-control skills and the additional skills detailed in the following chapter, that means you always should be on the lookout for what your players are doing *right*.

Rather than correct what your players are doing wrong, demonstrate to them how to do each skill the right way, and then praise whatever part of each skill they perform correctly when they try it. When you continue to see your players performing parts or all of a skill incorrectly, don't tell them what you're seeing. Instead, offer thoughtful suggestions for improvement—between large ladlefuls of continued praise for their efforts.

ers, on a one-on-one basis, how to perform the skill correctly. Then it's up to you to warmly praise your players' efforts as they gradually become more proficient at each skill.

Skill 1: Dribbling with the Inside of the Foot and Stopping the Ball by Stepping on It

Beginning young soccer players know only two speeds, full out and dead stop. Unfortunately, neither of these speeds is the norm for the majority of play in soccer.

If players don't move on the soccer field, they'll obviously lose every game they ever play. If they sprint full out every second of every game, they'll collapse from exhaustion before halftime. Moreover, when players dribble at full speed, they must concentrate on maintaining control of the ball. That means they must constantly look down and can run in only one direction.

Rarely do soccer players stop or sprint flat out with the ball. Instead, the game of soccer is played mostly at intermediate speed as players move the ball, pass the ball, and jockey for position with the ball. At intermediate speed, players are able to look around and see the rest of the field while they maintain control of the ball. Only in so doing can they spot open players and complete passes to them.

"Touching and moving the ball in search of attacking and scoring opportunities—that's the heart of soccer in twelve words."

As players grow competent at dribbling the ball at intermediate speed, they do so without looking at the ball at all. Instead, they touch and move the ball while keeping it in their peripheral vision, all the while studying the playing field for attacking and scoring opportunities.

Touching and moving the ball in search of attacking and scoring opportunities—that's the heart of soccer in twelve words. And that explains why you should teach your players, as the first soccer skill they ever learn, how to dribble at intermediate speed while maintaining control of the ball.

How to Dribble

The simplest way to dribble the ball under control at intermediate speed is to jog straight ahead while alternately touching the ball—and thus moving the ball a few feet ahead—with the inside of the left and right foot.

Before your first practice, try dribbling correctly yourself:

- Stand with the ball at your feet
- Lightly kick the ball with the inside of your right foot and jog along behind the ball at a leisurely pace
- When you catch up with the still-moving ball, repeat the light kick with your left foot and continue jogging

You'll quickly establish a rhythm whereby you'll kick the ball with one foot, jog two steps, then kick it again with your other foot. (Though not crucial, alternating feet makes finding that rhythm easier.)

As you dribble, the ball never should be more than 1 to 2 yards in front of you. If the ball is farther from you than that, it easily will be tackled, or stolen, by your opponent.

In addition, the ball never should be directly beneath your body. If you end up with the ball between your feet, you'll either trip over the ball or strike it with too much force.

To come to a stop, simply catch up with the ball and step on it lightly with the bottom of either foot.

How to Teach Dribbling

To start off your first practice, have your players try dribbling.

First, set up a driving-lanes grid and a rectangular practice grid before practice.

Using the Easter egg trick (see page 67), arrange half your players, up to six total, in their driving lanes with their balls at their feet in front of them. (The other half of your team will be in the rectangular practice grid with your parent helper performing another drill, as assigned for each practice session in the final chapter of this book.)

Now it's time for you to talk to your players. Remember: No lectures.

Begin with a quick story to pique their interest. The story you choose isn't important. Rather, what's important is for you to involve your players in a miniature story line, in a plot, in an *adventure*. For example, you might tell your players that they're truck drivers, that the soccer ball is their precious cargo, and that thieves are waiting along the road to steal it. Add excitement to your story by working your eyebrows, widening your eyes, and speaking in a funny-serious manner. Emphasize to your players that they must drive cautiously, keeping their cargo only a few feet ahead of them at all times to keep the thieves from stealing it.

That's just one story from among many possibilities. Tell your players whatever story you wish. The key is to limit your story to only two or three sentences and to have your story augment the skill you're teaching.

Next, tell your players what you want them to do. In this case, when you shout, "Green light!" they are to jog ahead slowly, kicking the ball ahead of them. When you yell, "Red light!" they are to come to a stop by stepping on the ball with one foot.

Now holler out "Green light!" to send them off.

Some of your players will take off at a wild sprint, kicking the ball far out in front of them. Others will kick the ball timidly, and the ball will roll only a few inches. Those who weren't listening will take note of what their teammates are doing and will follow suit.

Quickly now, holler "Red light!" It'll take a while for your players to catch up to the ball and place one foot atop it, but eventually they'll manage to do so. The instant all of them do, shout "Green light!" again.

When your players reach the end of their driving lanes, instruct them to turn around and head back the way they came.

Dribbling with Inside of Foot

Proper dribbling with inside of foot

Not with the toes

Now is when you become a teacher. As you continue the drill by alternately hollering out "Red light!" and "Green light!" come up alongside your players one at a time and offer advice, based on the technical description above, and using elements of your story line if you wish, to encourage your players to correctly dribble the ball at intermediate speed.

When you give feedback to your players, be sure to praise all the things they're doing correctly, such as:

- Striking the ball with the forward half of the inside of the foot, not with their toes (see diagram)
- Jogging, as opposed to either sprinting or walking
- Keeping the ball a yard or two in front of them
- Using alternating feet to strike the ball
- Stopping with the bottom of the foot—not their toes or heel—resting on the ball

When you praise those players who are dribbling and stopping the ball correctly, players in the other lanes will hear you. In search of praise themselves, they'll begin performing certain parts of the skill correctly as well.

Move from player to player as you continue to shout "Red light!" and "Green light!" Offer lots of praise and no more than one constructive suggestion—"Be sure to keep the ball close in front of you, Karen, so the thieves won't be able to steal your cargo"—per player.

End the drill after 5 minutes or so, or when your players begin to grow restless. The rest of the 10-minute time period allotted for the drill will be

Emily pushes the ball with the inside of her foot. (1)

Emily keeps the ball close and in control. (2)

taken up by switching squads back and forth, and by the end-of-drill water break.

You might or might not have time to work with all your players during the 5 minutes you run the drill. Either way, don't worry about it. By repeating the Red Light/Green Light drill at the beginning of every practice, you'll have ample opportunity in future practice sessions to work adequately with all your players.

Praise your players' efforts and offer a quick closing to your story: "Great work, truckers! You did such a good job moving your cargo that I'm certain no thieves were able to get away with any of it. Way to go!"

Now have the players in the driving lanes trade with the players in the rectangular grid and repeat the introduction of the skill with the other half of your players.

What to Look For

Remember, your players won't come anywhere close to mastering this skill—or any of the other five skills—the first time they try it. Your goal is simply to get them performing the skill. Most problems your players have with each skill will tend to correct themselves through repetition over time. In addition, your moving among your players each time you play Red Light/Green Light, offering lots of praise and one suggestion for improvement per player, also will help them master each skill.

Here are the most common problems your players will have with dribbling and stopping the ball:

1. Kicking the ball with their toes. Encourage your players to strike the ball with the forward half of the inside of the foot. You may even need to get down on your knees and press the inside of a player's foot against the ball to show him exactly how he is to strike the ball.
2. Dribbling too fast. Try imitating the sound of a police siren and handing out a pretend warning for speeding as a fun way to suggest that a player slow down. Better yet, loudly praise those players who are dribbling at the correct speed and, as a result, are able to keep an eye out for thieves.
3. Dribbling too slowly. Encourage players to keep the ball moving. Explain that it isn't necessary for the ball to come to a complete stop before they kick it again.
4. Striking the ball too hard. Explain that the thieves will steal the players' precious cargo if they kick it too far out in front of them.
5. Tripping over the ball. Explain to your players that they should be reaching ahead slightly with their feet each time they strike the ball. Why? Because that's how truckers make their deliveries on time.

Skill 2: Dribbling with Speed

When there is open space on the field through which your players should move quickly, or when your players get around and ahead of their opponents in a breakaway situation, they'll need to be able to dribble the ball under control, but as fast as they can possibly go. In addition, when a player attempts to dribble around someone, she'll usually "cut," or turn, the ball, then apply a burst of speed to get around and beyond the opponent while still maintaining control of the ball. If she doesn't speed up after cutting the ball, her opponent will simply catch up with her and thwart her attack.

Devin dribbles with speed.

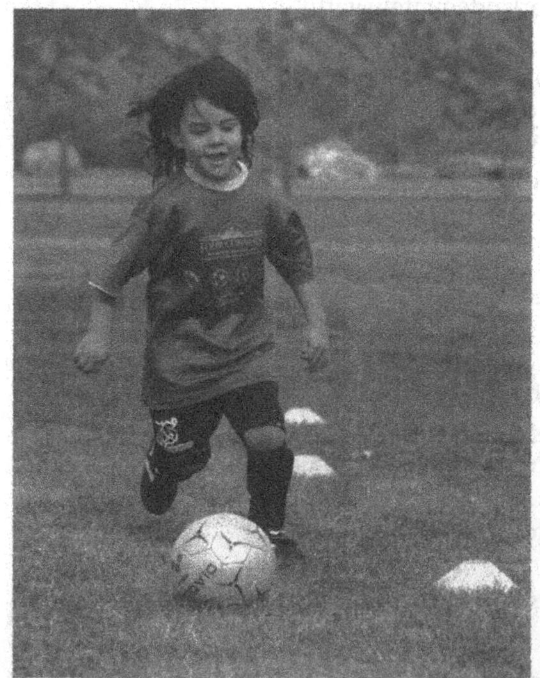

Speeding up, and maintaining that higher speed with the ball, is what makes attacking and scoring soccer goals possible—and is therefore the second skill your players should learn.

How to Dribble with Speed

When advanced players dribble as fast as they can go, they strike the ball with the outside of their feet. Eventually, your players will do the same. It's impossible for 6-and-under players to master that technique, however. Instead, young players simply need to learn how to make the switch from jogging at intermediate speed and keeping the ball only 1 or 2 yards in front of them to running full out and striking the ball hard enough that it extends up to 3 or 4 yards ahead of them with each kick.

To do that, your players will need to reach forward with their feet and push or kick the ball ahead with the laces of their shoes.

Why the laces? Stop and think about what's happening for a moment.

Your players have sped up. That means that when they strike the ball with their feet, they'll unavoidably do so with more force.

Your players won't strike the ball with the insides of their feet when they're running flat out. It's simply impossible to run full speed and, at the same time, turn the foot out to strike the ball with the inside of the foot. Instead, when they accelerate to full speed, your players will be tempted to strike the ball with their toes. Only the best soccer players in the world can control kicks they make with their toes. For the rest of us—including your players—toe kicks result in errant, hard-struck balls.

In contrast, the laces cover the instep—the broadest part of the foot. When your players push the ball with their laces while running flat out, they strike the ball with the least amount of force—and therefore the most control—possible.

At about age 7, some of your players naturally—and correctly—will begin using the outsides of their feet to push the ball forward as they run flat out with the ball. They'll do so because using the outside of the foot is the most efficient way to maintain full speed while moving the ball. At about the same age, other players can be taught this skill. For now, however, your goal is simply to get your players to accelerate with the ball and, when they do, to switch from striking the ball with the inside of the foot to striking the ball with the laces.

How to Teach Dribbling with Speed

You'll introduce this skill at the start of your second practice with half, or up to six, of your players lined up in their Red Light/Green Light driving lanes. Now's your chance to continue your story theme. If your players are "truckers" working to avoid losing their cargo—their soccer balls—to thieves, you can explain to them that they must speed up as fast as they can go to outrun the thieves when they "hit the highway."

Now tell them what you want them to do: When you say, "Green light!" they are to begin dribbling, kicking the ball just ahead of them, with the inside of the foot, at intermediate speed. When you shout, "Hit the highway!" they are to speed up until they are running as fast as they can, pushing the ball farther ahead of them with the shoelaces. When you call, "Red light!" they are to stop with the ball beneath one foot, as they did the previous practice.

Holler "Green light!" to get your players moving, and then quickly yell "Hit the highway!" Chaos will ensue. Toes will strike balls, which will shoot away in all directions. Assuming you've brought the right attitude to practice and have begun to instill it in your players, all will be well.

Yell "Red light!" to get your players to chase down their balls and

Pushing versus Kicking the Ball

You may have noticed we've used the term *pushing* rather than *kicking* the ball when discussing how best to move the ball ahead while running full speed. That's because when soccer players run flat out with the ball, they don't really kick it at all. They're moving so fast that if they were to actually kick the ball, it would shoot far out in front of them, and they would lose control of it.

Your young players gradually will learn through repetition that they must only *push* the ball ahead of them with their laces if they are to maintain control of the ball while running full speed, just as older players push the ball ahead of them with the outsides of their feet when they run flat out.

Dribbling with speed: the toes are pointed down, and the player reaches to **push** the ball with the laces.

come to a stop. Now yell "Green light!" to get them to return to their lanes. As soon as they're back in their lanes, remind them to try to push the ball ahead with their shoelaces when they speed up, and then immediately shout "Hit the highway!"

More chaos, more grins, and more fun will ensue. And very quickly your players will begin to accelerate while keeping the ball under control. Each time one of your players manages to do so, offer lots of praise. As you continue to call out traffic signals and your players continue to move the ball erratically up and down their lanes, walk among them as you did the previous practice. This time, keep an eye out for things your players are doing right and wrong with both skills—dribbling and stopping the ball, and dribbling with speed. Offer up praise, encouragement, and only one suggestion per player per practice session.

End the drill after several minutes, when you've had the chance to visit with some or all of your players individually. Tell your winded players what a great job they did outrunning the thieves by "hitting the highway" with so much speed, exchange a few high fives with the nearest players, and then switch with the other half of your team and repeat the drill.

What to Look For

1. Kicking the ball with their toes. Just as with dribbling at intermediate speed, your players will tend to kick the ball with their toes when you first tell them to "hit the highway."

The problem with the front end of the foot, the toes, is that this end is pointed. If a player doesn't strike the ball perfectly—a virtual certainty—there's no telling where the ball will go. Yet, by instinct, the first thing all kids try to do when they take to a soccer field is kick the ball with their toes.

Encourage your players to use the insides of their feet to move the ball a short distance ahead when dribbling at intermediate speed, and to use their laces to push the ball farther ahead of them when they "hit the highway" and accelerate to full speed.

Offer praise to those who push and move the ball correctly, offer gentle suggestions to those who continue to kick with their toes—and understand that toe kicking is, inevitably, a part of 6-and-under soccer.

2. Allowing the ball to fall back between their legs. When your players hear the words "hit the highway," they'll be so excited to take off running that they'll often forget to push the ball along with them. The ball will slow and fall back between their legs, at which point they'll trip over it and tumble to the ground.

   In response, explain to those players that when they speed up, they should try to keep the ball so far out in front of them that they almost have to lunge or take a big step forward each time they strike it. "That's the only way to keep your cargo safely with you while you try to outrun the highway robbers," you can tell them.

Skill 3: Changing Direction with the Inside of the Foot, or "Cutting" the Ball

The first two skills, dribbling and dribbling with speed, are about moving the ball in one direction. A large part of soccer, however, is about *changing direction* with the ball. That fact goes right back to watching what the pros do. The first touches you'll see any professional soccer player make on a ball after receiving a pass have to do with changing the ball's direction. The pro might angle the ball to the right or left or even move the ball backward—whatever is necessary for him to get where he wants to go with the ball.

Now consider one of your young players. When she has the ball in her possession during a game, most likely she'll have an opponent between her and the goal. The only way for your player to get around that opponent is by changing directions with the ball.

Note that for your player to move around her opponent, she'll need to "cut" or change the direction of the ball to her right or left. Then, when clear of her opponent, she'll need to cut the ball back in the direction of the goal once again. Essentially your player will need to perform at least two significant changes of direction on her ball to get around each opponent she faces.

Most cuts, whether performed by beginning or advanced players, involve changing the direction of the ball 90 degrees or less because a cut of more than 90 degrees means the player is moving the ball away from the goal she is attacking. You, however, will be teaching your players to perform

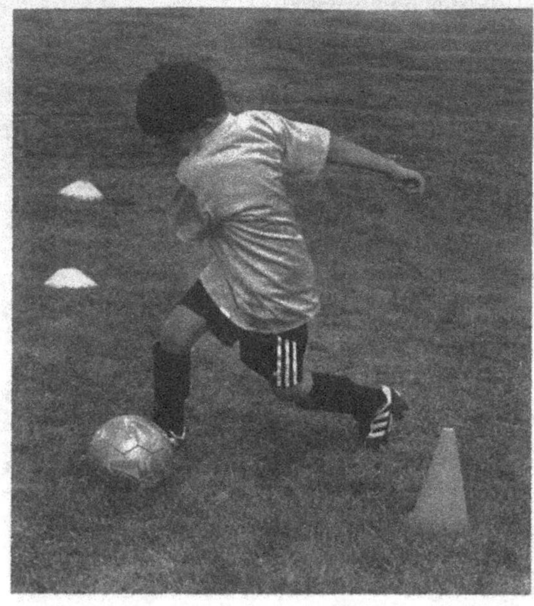

Kele cuts the ball.

a series of cuts on the ball to change the direction of the ball's travel a full 180 degrees. Turns of 180 degrees, accomplished with a series of lesser cuts to the ball, work within the confines of the Red Light/Green Light driving lanes and so enable your players to develop the skill of cutting the ball on their own under your close and direct supervision.

Because your players' 180-degree turns of the ball will be accomplished with a series of lesser-degree cuts, the skill your players develop to accomplish such turns will transfer directly to the soccer field on game days. In addition, changing the ball's direction a full 180 degrees is far more difficult than simply changing the ball's direction to a lesser degree. When your players have mastered the ability to cut the ball enough times to change its direction a full 180 degrees within the confines of their Red Light/Green Light driving lanes, they'll be able to change the ball's direction 90 degrees or less on the soccer field with ease.

Many coaches teach the performance of lesser-degree cuts by having their players kick the ball around and around in a figure eight or along a winding cone slalom course. Unlike the fun and excitement of Red Light/Green Light, such repetitious drills are boring and therefore not well suited to soccer players of any age, much less those 6 and under.

How to Cut the Ball

The first thing a soccer player must do when preparing to change the ball's direction is get both feet to one side of the ball. If the player wants to turn the ball to the left, he must get his left foot out of the way—that is, get both feet to the right of the ball. Likewise, he must get his right foot out of the way of the ball before he can turn the ball to the right.

Cutting the Ball

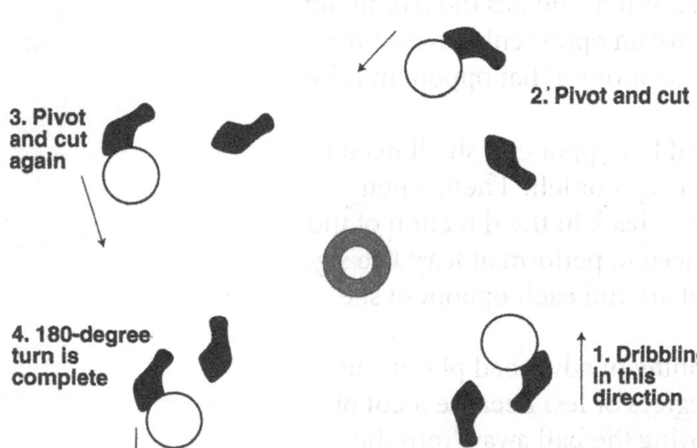
2. Pivot and cut
3. Pivot and cut again
4. 180-degree turn is complete
1. Dribbling in this direction

Next, the player must plant the foot he moves out of the way in a pivoted, or angled, position that is aimed halfway in the direction he wants to cut the ball. For example, to turn or cut the ball 90 degrees to the left, the player must plant his left foot just behind and to the right of the ball with his toes pointing at the ball and his foot angled at 45 degrees—half the 90 degrees he plans to turn the ball.

Next, the player must come across the ball with his right foot in front of his left. His right foot must then strike the ball with the forward half of the inside of his foot, sending the ball off at a 90-degree angle from the direction it formerly was traveling.

How to Teach Cutting

You'll need to add a single cone in the middle of each driving lane to begin teaching your players to cut the ball as part of the Red Light/Green Light drill at the start of your third practice. Your players are in their driving lanes, with a soccer ball at their feet. Tell them they're going to have to turn their trucks tightly around the cone in the middle of the lane in order to avoid the thieves waiting up ahead.

Tell your players to move with the ball at intermediate speed when you call out "Green light!" They are to turn the ball around the cone in the lane and return to the starting position when you yell "Roundabout!"

Send your players off with a call of "Green light!" Then, when your players near their cones—some, obviously, will arrive more quickly than others—yell "Roundabout!"

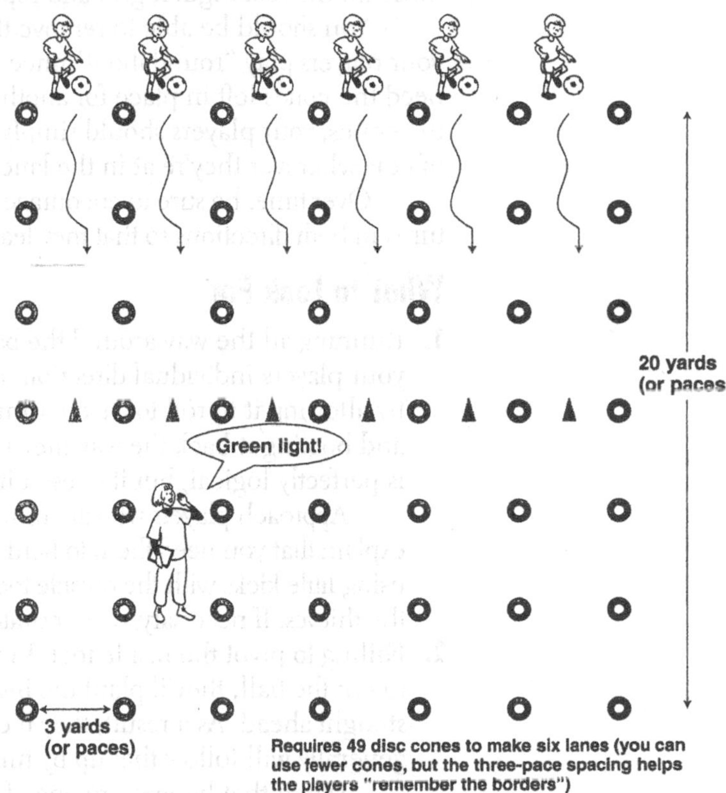
Green light!
20 yards
(or paces
3 yards
(or paces)
Requires 49 disc cones to make six lanes (you can use fewer cones, but the three-pace spacing helps the players "remember the borders")

Grid for Cutting the Ball

Eventually your players will return to their starting points with their soccer balls. When that happens, call out "Green light!" and repeat the process. After a few rounds, your players will understand what they're supposed to do—kick the ball up the lane, around the cone, and back to the starting position. At that point you'll be able to work your way from player to player, teaching them *how* to do what they're doing.

Much of how to cut the ball will come naturally to your players—moving the inside leg out of the way, pointing the inside foot at the ball, sweeping across the body with the outside leg to strike the ball with the inside of the foot. When your players get it right, praise them. When they don't, offer suggestions to help them out.

While concentrating on having your players cut the ball, don't forget to call out "Hit the highway!" and "Red light!" a couple of times to add variety and fun to the drill, and to enable your players to practice their other skills along with cutting the ball.

When you've gotten the chance to work with several of your players, end the drill with praise and a comment about how well they did turning their cargo away from the thieves. Then switch this group of players with those on the rectangular grid and repeat the drill.

You should be able to remove the cones from the driving lanes after your players play "roundabout" once. Very young players, however, may need the cones left in place for another practice or two. After you remove the cones, your players should simply turn the ball 180 degrees with a series of cuts wherever they're at in the lane each time you call "Roundabout!"

Over time, be sure to encourage your players to perform their 180-degree turns in both directions so that they learn to cut the ball with either foot.

What to Look For

1. Running all the way around the ball. Before you have the chance to offer your players individual direction, many will turn the ball around simply by allowing it to roll to a stop, running around to the far side of the ball, and booting it back the way they just came. Such action by your players is perfectly logical, but it doesn't involve cutting the ball.

   Approach players who are using this technique to "turn" the ball and explain that you need them to herd the ball around their cones quickly, using little kicks with the outside foot, in order to keep their cargo away from the thieves. If necessary, demonstrate to them what you want them to do.
2. Failing to pivot the inside foot. In many cases when your players first try to cut the ball, they'll plant the inside foot on the ground still pointing straight ahead. As a result, they'll end up knocking the ball erratically and generally will follow that up by tumbling to the ground in a heap.

   When that happens to one of your players, help her to her feet and demonstrate the way she must get her inside leg out of the way and pivot her inside foot so as to enable her outside foot to swing across and strike the ball. Once you've demonstrated the need to get the inside leg out of the way a couple of times, she'll begin to understand it.
3. Touching the ball too many times. To start out, your young players may need to touch, or cut, the ball a dozen or more times to turn it a full 180 degrees. That number will decrease dramatically over time. Try suggesting to those who continue to touch the ball numerous times as they make their turns that they point their toes farther to the inside with each touch, and that they count how few touches they can use to accomplish turning the ball.

Skill 4: The Pull Turn

Now for a short respite from the chaos you'll face teaching your players to cut the ball and dribble with speed.

The pull turn is a skill worth learning because it introduces the use of the bottom of the foot as a way of *moving* the ball as opposed to just *stopping* the ball. It's also a skill many of your players will master fairly quickly.

George initiates a pull turn. (1)

George pivots with the ball. (2)

George completes his pull turn. (3)

You'll be teaching your players the 180-degree pull turn, wherein your players will stop the ball with the bottom of their foot and pull the ball back the way they've just come. In game situations, however, your players eventually will use modified versions of the pull turn. Advanced players will stop the ball and slightly change its direction by rolling it beneath their foot. Rather than perform a full, 180-degree pull turn, they'll pull the ball backward or roll it from side to side in order to outwit an opponent. They'll then accelerate and dribble away in a new direction with the ball, leaving the opponent behind.

Such slight ball-direction pull turns are too difficult for your young players to master. Instead, learning the full, 180-degree pull turn will serve as a great precursor to the lesser, fancy-footwork pull turns they'll use on the soccer field in the years ahead.

How to Perform the Pull Turn

The 180-degree pull turn is a fairly straightforward skill. While dribbling the ball in one direction, the player performs four simple motions. He:

- Stops the ball by stepping on it with the bottom of his foot
- Pulls the ball backward beneath his foot so that it rolls back past him

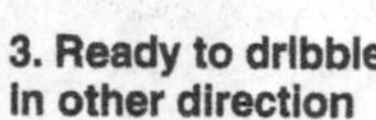

3. Ready to dribble in other direction 2. Pull back and pivot toward the ball 1. Foot and eyes on the ball

Pull Turn: Correct

- Turns to face the ball as he executes the change of direction with it
- Dribbles the ball away in the opposite direction

How to Teach the Pull Turn

Your players are poised and ready in their Red Light/Green Light driving lanes for the start of your fourth practice. Continue your story theme by, for example, explaining that your players again must outwit the robbers waiting along the highway by quickly turning around with their cargo. Next, tell them that when you call out "U-turn!" they should stop the ball with the bottom of one foot, pull the ball back past their bodies, and dribble back the way they've just come. Quickly call out "Green light!" to get them dribbling and then yell "U-turn!"

Because your players will be stopping the ball before changing direction, not as much chaos will ensue as with cutting the ball. Still, confusion will be rampant. Repeat your calls a few times, from "Green light!" to "U-turn!" and back to "Green light!" as you work your way among your players, complimenting their progress and offering suggestions.

Just as your players begin to get the idea of the pull turn figured out—and just when there's so little chaos in the driving lanes that you can barely stand it—shout "Roundabout!"

Chaos will reign once again.

When your players manage their cut turns, shout "Green light!" followed by a quick "Hit the highway!"

Your players will have been concentrating so hard on the pull turn that they'll have forgotten all about using their laces to dribble with speed. Instead, they'll revert to booting the ball with their toes as they take off at a sprint. As soccer balls spurt in all directions, your players will knock into one another and trip and fall. Ahhh—more chaos.

When, eventually, your players return to the driving lanes with their balls, run them through a few more "U-turns!" as you walk among them, and then switch to the other half of your team and repeat the activity.

Pull Turn: Incorrect

2. Turns in wrong direction, loses sight of the ball 1. Pulls ball back

What to Look For

1. Turning away from the ball. The one problem your players will face as they try the pull turn is the tendency to spin away from the ball after they pull it backward.

To you or any other adult, it makes obvious sense that once you've pulled the ball back past your body to initiate a pull turn, you should naturally turn with the ball, tracking it with your eyes and pivoting your body, before dribbling the ball away in the opposite direction. But that logic doesn't hold with 6-and-under players.

When your players attempt their first pull turns, more than half will spin *away* from the ball after they pull it backward. They'll begin pivoting their bodies with the ball in order to pull it back past themselves. Then they'll stop that pivot and instead pivot, or spin, all the way around the other way, losing sight of the ball in the process, before trying to relocate the ball again and, upon eventually doing so, dribbling away in the opposite direction.

Kele demonstrates incorrectly pivoting away from the ball during a pull turn.

Maybe it's the natural desire to dance that resides in all 6-and-under kids that causes so many to spin wildly away from the ball as part of their 180-degree pull turns. Who knows? All we know is that you'll need to encourage your kids to pivot *with* the ball as they complete their pull turns—correctly using their bodies to shield their "cargo" from the "highway robbers" as they do so—rather than pivot *away* from the ball and momentarily losing sight and control of their precious cargo in the process.

2. Using the heel of the foot to stop the ball and initiate the pull turn. Young players who reach far out and attempt to stop the ball and initiate pull turns with their heel will be so out of balance that they'll be as apt to fall to the ground as to complete their turns. Instead, players should use the bottom of their foot when stopping the ball and performing pull turns.

   As you call out "U-turn! and move among your players, praise those using the bottom of their foot correctly, and encourage the rest to follow suit.

3. Using their toes to stop the ball and initiate the pull turn. In this common case, the ball is too far forward on the foot. When the player pulls back on the ball, her foot immediately slips off it and the ball doesn't go anywhere. As with using the heel, encourage your players to use the bottom of their foot to stop the ball and pull it backward.

Skill 5: Receiving the Ball

If the lack of chaos while teaching your players the pull turn made your life as a 6-and-under soccer coach too easy, don't despair. The final two skills will add all the chaos to your practices you could ever hope for. It's worth it, however, in terms of what your players will gain from practicing these skills, both of which will set them on the path to fully and ably *controlling* the ball.

Skill 5 involves teaching your players to receive, or settle, balls that are passed to them in the air, whether by their own players or, just as likely at this age, their opponents. For many years, the term *trap* was used to describe the process of receiving a pass and settling, or calming, the ball so that it could be dribbled and played by the receiving player. However, as the game of soccer has grown increasingly sophisticated in recent years, the term *trap*—with its connotations of stopping and ensnaring the ball—has fallen from favor. Instead, the term *receive* has grown in favor because the term more accurately describes how today's talented players control the ball when it's passed to them in the air, and how they direct the ball's onward movement without actually bringing it to a complete stop by *trapping* it with their feet.

Receiving a pass and moving the ball onward is a critical component of soccer. That's why we include it as one of the basic ball-control skills you'll be teaching your players. The reality, however, is that you won't really be teaching your 6-and-under players how to receive a ball from the air while on the move. Rather, as out of favor as the word *trap* may be with soccer sophisticates, *trapping* the ball is exactly what you'll be teaching your players to do.

Admittedly, the ball isn't kicked up in the air much during 6-and-under soccer games. Still, this skill will help your players master eye-foot coordination and will prepare them for the day when the ball will be played in the air frequently. Eventually, of course—when they have won their college soccer scholarships or have turned pro—all your former players will be able to receive 50-yard punts from their goalkeepers with amazing flicks of their feet that will redirect those punts with concise accuracy and lead to devastating attacks. That's only obvious. To begin with, though, your young players must simply learn to stop the ball when it comes to them in the air. They must learn to *receive* balls by *trapping* them with their feet.

How to Receive the Ball

First, let's confess right up front that teaching your players to control the ball in their individual driving lanes, as part of the Red Light/Green Light drill, involves having your players touch the ball with their hands. Yet your goal as a coach is to get your players to touch and move the ball with their feet as much as possible.

What gives?

Frankly, what gives is the fact that 6-and-under players best learn to receive the ball in the air and juggle the ball *on their own*.

Curtis "traps" the ball.

Countless 6-and-under coaches teach their players to receive passes by lining up their players opposite one another and having them pass the ball back and forth to one another. This drill works quite well for teaching kids to make and receive passes on the ground—the primary way your 6-and-under players will receive the ball during their games. It is, however, deadly boring. That's why we eschew that drill and recommend you do the same. Instead, you'll have great success teaching your players to receive the ball in the air—or *settle* or *trap* the ball—by having them throw the ball up in the air, then step on it as quickly as possible when it falls to the ground.

It's a matter of making a trade-off. Yes, you'll be directing your players to touch the ball with their hands. As a result, however, your players will learn to control the ball from the air as part of the Red Light/Green Light drill. That means they'll have *fun* while they learn the skill, and so they'll continue to enjoy the game of soccer. To us, that trade-off clearly is worth making.

Technically what you'll want your players to do is pick the ball up, throw it in the air head high, and use eye-foot coordination to step on it so that it bounces once off the ground and hits the bottom of one foot, which then will settle atop the ball, trapping it against the ground. (See photos.)

How to Teach Receiving

With your players at ready in their Red Light/Green Light driving lanes at the start of this, your fifth practice, continue your story by, for example, explaining that, as truckers, they must receive incoming cargo with their feet no matter where it comes from—in this case, the sky. Go on to explain that when you shout "Out of the sky!" your players are to stop the ball with the bottom of one foot, pick it up with their hands, and toss it straight up in the air just above their heads. As the ball falls to the ground, they are to move one foot over it and trap the ball against the ground as quickly as they can.

Send them off with a quick "Green light!" then follow up with a "Red light!" and an "Out of the sky!"

When chaos erupts once more, as it assuredly will, remember that mastering this skill requires your players to take their still-nascent eye-foot coordination skills to a new level. How many children catch a baseball the first time one is thrown to them? The same holds true for receiving, or trapping, a soccer ball—except that success is even more elusive because receiving a soccer ball must be done with the feet.

Move among your players as you call "Out of the sky!" Offer praise and suggestions as you go. Be sure to include your other traffic signals as well. After a few minutes, switch your player groups and repeat the activity.

What to Look For

1. Stopping after trapping the ball. The tendency among your players will be to stop moving and proudly stand with one foot on the ball each time they perform a successful trap. However, the act of trapping the ball is simply a step along the way toward truly receiving a punted or passed ball on the fly. To get your players moving toward that future, encourage them to get moving by dribbling on up their driving lanes as soon as they successfully trap the ball.
2. Not raising the foot high enough, or stepping on the ball too hard. In these cases, the ball is likely to bounce away, or the player may fall to the ground.

   Explain that the player should think not of stepping on the *ground*, but of lifting his foot high enough to step lightly down on the *ball*.
3. Ongoing difficulties with the skill, as well as quick mastery of it. Some of your players will have great difficulty trapping the ball. Suggest to any such players that they drop the ball from the waist rather than tossing the ball in the air head high.

   Other players will master the trap quickly. You might want to suggest to a player who has mastered the against-the-ground trap that he try to receive, or trap, his ball by slowing, catching, and ultimately controlling the ball with the top of his foot. Instinct will tell him he should cup his foot by pulling his toes back to cradle the ball. You'll need to point out that, in fact, to successfully catch and control his ball before it strikes the ground, he must raise his foot with his toes outstretched. Then explain that, as the ball descends, he must drop his foot to cushion the ball, slow its descent, and catch it.

Skill 6: Juggling the Ball

Nothing does more to improve kids' ball-control skills than juggling the ball. *Nothing.*

The simple act of trying to keep the ball in the air for as long as possible by bouncing it off the feet, chest, and thighs teaches young players the elusive but all-important ability known as *ball sense.*

The older players get, the more the ball is played in the air during games. An advanced player will juggle the ball as part of her game-play tactics. She'll receive a pass against her chest, drop the ball to her foot, and pop it past her opponent before the ball even hits the ground—but she'll only be able to do so if she is a talented juggler.

Teaching players to juggle when they are young introduces them to the concept of playing the ball in the air. Much more important for now, however, is the fact that, by becoming competent jugglers—that is, by learning to dribble in the air—young players will be that much better at dribbling the ball on the ground.

Your hope for your players should be that one day all of them will have tremendous ball sense—that they'll be able to dribble and change direction without looking down at the ball, that they'll receive and control long passes with ease, that they'll have mastered the basic skills that will enable them to be truly creative on the soccer field.

What one single thing can you do to help your players get there from where they're at today? Start them juggling now, and encourage them to keep at it as long as they play soccer.

How to Juggle the Ball

Juggling is nothing more—or less—than keeping the ball in the air for as long as possible by bouncing it off any part of the body other than the hands and arms. Some soccer experts compare juggling to dribbling in the air. When you're dribbling in the air as opposed to on the ground, you don't have the friction of the ground to slow the ball, which means your *feel* for the ball—your ball sense—must be that much finer to maintain *control* of the ball.

Older soccer players begin juggling by flipping the ball into the air with their feet. From there they attempt to keep the ball off the ground by lightly kicking or striking the ball to bat it back in the air with the body parts of their choice, from foot to forehead to shoulder to thigh, and on and on. Talented soccer players are capable of juggling balls indefinitely, even while carrying on a conversation. Your goal for your players, however, is simply to have them learn to drop the ball from their hands, strike the ball one time with their feet, and catch the ball again.

Note that it's easier for your players to begin juggling by holding the ball out before them, dropping it, and first trying to bounce the ball off their thighs. Despite this fact, we recommend young players begin juggling by

Devin (left) and Leo (right) give juggling a try.

dropping the ball to their feet because the game of soccer is all about using the feet to control and move the ball. The thighs come into play during soccer games far less often. By teaching your players to begin juggling with their feet, you'll enable them to become better soccer players faster than if you were to start them juggling with their thighs.

In order for your players to be successful juggling the ball with their feet, you'll need to instruct them to point their toes and strike the ball on their laces with their feet outstretched. Only then will they propel the ball straight up in the air so they can catch it.

How to Teach Juggling

With your players in their Red Light/Green Light driving lanes, tell them there are times when even the best drivers get stuck in traffic jams. Explain that you want them to juggle the ball by kicking it up in the air and catching it whenever you call out "Traffic jam!"

Send them off with "Green light!" Then shout "Red light!" followed by "Traffic jam!" When, as usual, chaos takes over, remember that it's absolutely worthwhile.

Move among your players as they attempt to juggle. Have each player hold the ball waist high at arm's length. Then instruct him to drop the ball and swing one leg up to meet the dropped ball, with his extended toe making the top of his foot parallel with the ground, enabling the ball to pop straight back up in the air so that he's able to catch it. The goal of each player should be to catch the ball after he strikes it one time.

Switch player groups with your parent helper and repeat the activity.

1. Hold ball waist high

2. Drop ball and kick with toes pointed, ball striking laces

Correct Juggling: Toes Pointed

What to Look For

1. Accepting the lack of prettiness and the potential for frustration. Expect that this drill will be horrendously messy and potentially frustrating to your players at first. But understand as well that learning to juggle is critical to your young players' future success. Offer lots of encouragement to your players. Feel free to level with them: tell them you know what you're asking of them is difficult, but explain that their attempts at juggling will make them fantastic soccer players, and that they should feel free to try juggling on their own time at home, too, if they wish.

   And be sure to use the "Traffic jam!" signal sparingly at first.
2. Swinging the leg fully extended at the ball. Your players should swing only their lower legs at the ball, popping the ball with their instep to propel the ball straight up into the air.
3. Not pointing their toes. If your players cup their feet rather than point their toes, the kicked ball will bounce right back into their faces.

   If players don't cup their feet but don't fully extend their toes either, the dropped ball will die rather than spring back in the air when it hits the foot because of the give inherent in the ankle of an unextended foot.

Incorrect Juggling: Toes Pulled Back

1. Hold ball waist high

2. Drop ball, holding leg straight with toes pulled back

Keep an eye out for these easy-to-miss problems and offer suggestions for improvement. Keep the faith. Your players will get it eventually, and when they do, the smiles on their faces will make all the failed attempts worthwhile.

CHAPTER 9

Eleven More Drills and Four More Skills

Quick Coaching Guide

Playing a variety of fun drills, or games, with your players will help them master ball movement and control through enjoyable repetition.

The best drills for 6-and-under players are 1) fun, 2) require helpful skill repetition, 3) encourage all participants to touch and move the ball most of the time, and 4) are either entirely noncompetitive or are flexible enough for you to increase or decrease the amount of competitiveness the drills entail.

In addition to the basic ball-control skills you'll introduce with the Red Light/Green Light drill, four additional skills—shooting, passing, receiving the ball on the ground, and shielding—are worth introducing to your young players with the drills detailed in this chapter.

The only way to master the basic ball-control skills detailed in the preceding chapter is through repetition. The easiest way to teach one of your players each skill would be to demonstrate the skill to her and have her repeat it several thousand times. But such an approach isn't for little kids—or anyone else, for that matter.

Instead, at the same time you're introducing basic ball-control skills to your players over the course of your first six practices, you'll reinforce those skills—and have your players repeat them many times over—by running your players through the additional eleven fun drills detailed in this chapter.

Remember, as far as your young players are concerned, you won't actually be running them through the following drills. You won't even be playing the following drills as "games" with them. Rather, you'll simply be involving them in story lines of your choosing, or those suggested below, because that's the best way to get your young players practicing, playing, and learning to love the game of soccer.

There are literally hundreds of great youth soccer drills. The twelve we've selected for you to teach your young players—Red Light/Green Light (in Chapter 8) and the eleven additional drills in this chapter—meet four strict criteria. Together those criteria make each of the twelve drills perfect for 6-and-under players. Every one of the drills:

1. Is, above all, *fun*.
2. Requires your players to repeat movements and actions aimed at helping them master basic ball-control skills.
3. Encourages all participants to touch and move their soccer balls most of the time.
4. Is either entirely noncompetitive or is flexible enough for you to increase or decrease the amount of competitiveness the drill entails.

Note that, like Drill 1: Red Light/Green Light, covered in the preceding chapter, the eleven additional drills you'll run with your players don't have winners and losers. Weaker players won't be winnowed out and forced to spend their valuable practice time sitting on the sidelines while stronger players continue to perform the drills, nor will scores be kept during the drills.

Unlike Red Light/Green Light, which is performed in the "driving lanes" grid, the eleven drills detailed in this chapter are performed in a practice grid 15 yards wide by 20 yards long.

Seven of the eleven drills are performed in an empty grid. Cones are placed haphazardly within the rectangular grid for Bulldozers and Builders, Alligator Pit, and Star Wars. A line of cones is set up within the grid for Trash Day. And four cones serve as goals at either end of the grid for Steal the Bacon.

Regular Grid

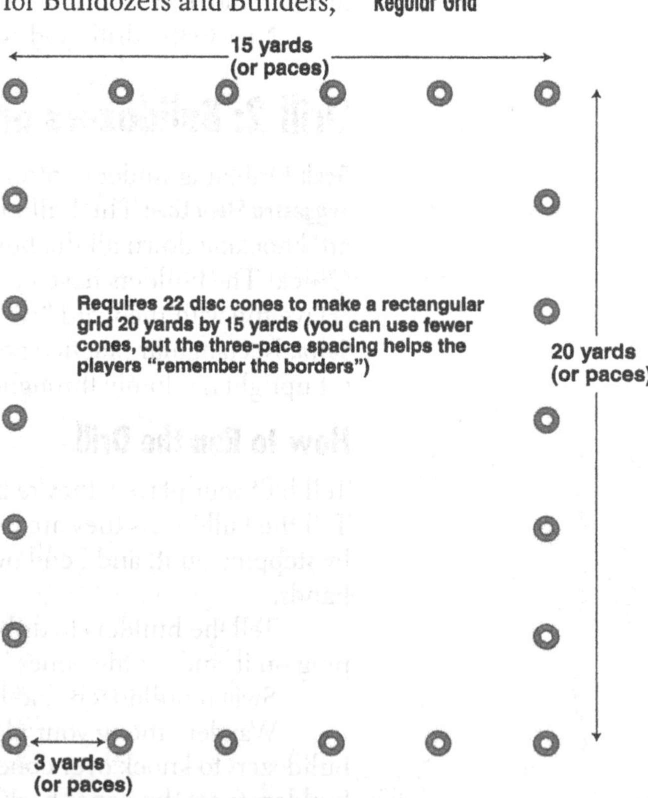
15 yards
(or paces)
Requires 22 disc cones to make a rectangular grid 20 yards by 15 yards (you can use fewer cones, but the three-pace spacing helps the players "remember the borders")
20 yards
(or paces)
3 yards
(or paces)

The eleven drills detailed in this chapter are presented in the order you'll introduce them to your players following Drill 1: Red Light/Green Light:

Drill 2: Bulldozers and Builders
Drill 3: Follow the Leader
Drill 4: Switch
Drill 5: Alligator Pit
Drill 6: Trash Day
Drill 7: Elmer Fudd
Drill 8: Star Wars
Drill 9: Crab Soccer
Drill 10: Sharks and Minnows
Drill 11: Steal the Bacon
Drill 12: Freeze Tag

In addition to the basic ball-control skills detailed in the preceding chapter, four additional, next-level skills—shooting, passing, receiving the ball on the ground, and shielding—are detailed in this chapter along with the drills that are most appropriate for introducing those skills. Shooting is covered with Drill 6: Trash Day; passing is taught with Drill 8: Star Wars; receiving the ball on the ground is dealt with in Drill 11: Steal the Bacon; and shielding is introduced with Drill 12: Freeze Tag.

As with the six ball-control skills we recommended you introduce to your players in the last chapter, there's no particular magic in the four additional, next-level skills we present in this chapter. Taken as a group, the four additional skills detailed here will enable your players to move forward as soccer players. Other skills could well do the same. The four we include here are simply those that are age-appropriate, and that we have found, over the years, most help young players improve their basic skills within the framework of the fun drills we suggest you run with your team.

Although mastery of the four additional skills presented in this chapter will help your players move to the next level in their development as soccer players, that mastery will not occur while your players are age 6 and under. Rather, the next-level skills we suggest you introduce to your young players are presented here simply so that you can *begin* introducing them to your players as they become ready to learn them, and as you have the opportunity to teach them.

Now to the drills and additional skills.

Drill 2: Bulldozers and Builders

Goal: Dribbling under control and stopping.
Suggested Story Line: The bulldozers are going *crrraaazzzyyy!!!* The bulldozers are knocking down all the buildings! (The cones are the "buildings.") Quick! Quick! The builders have to set the buildings back up as fast as they can! (Have fun with the word "crazy." Get *silly*. Your players will love it.)
Setup: Rectangular practice grid (22 disc cones) with at least 10 upright cones set upright randomly throughout.

How to Run the Drill

Tell half your players they're bulldozers and the other half they're builders. Tell the bulldozers they are to dribble the ball to upright cones, stop the ball by stepping on it, and bend over and knock down the cones with their hands.

Tell the builders to dribble to the toppled cones, stop the ball by stepping on it, and set the cones back upright with their hands.

Switch bulldozers and builders after 2 or 3 minutes.

Wander among your players as they perform the drill. Encourage the bulldozers to knock over cones as quickly as they can. Encourage the builders to set the cones back up as quickly as possible. Offer praise and sug-

Bulldozers and Builders

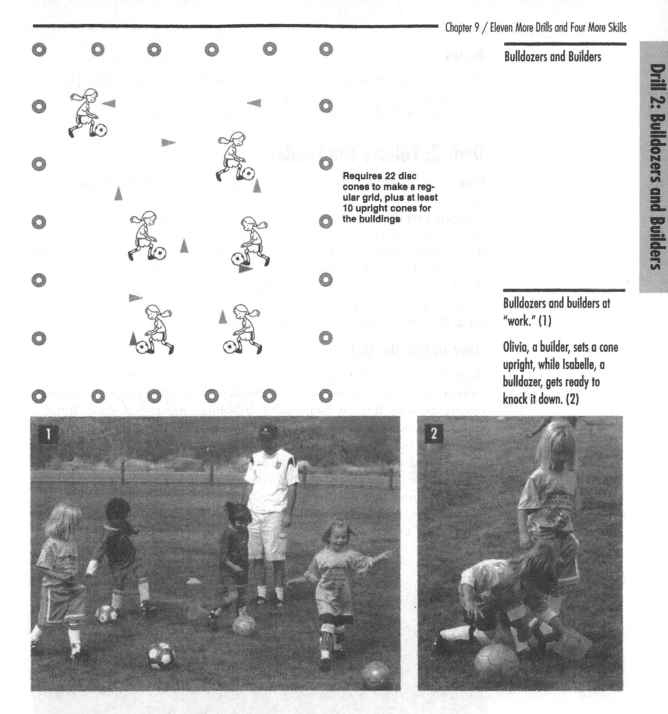

Requires 22 disc cones to make a regular grid, plus at least 10 upright cones for the buildings

Bulldozers and builders at "work." (1)

Olivia, a builder, sets a cone upright, while Isabelle, a bulldozer, gets ready to knock it down. (2)

gestions regarding your players' dribbling and ball-stopping techniques, as detailed in the preceding chapter.

Build on your story line throughout the drill: "Oh no! The buildings are almost all knocked over! Hurry, builders, hurry!" Or "Uh oh! Looks like the bulldozers are running out of gas! The builders have everything rebuilt already! Hurry, bulldozers, hurry!"

Notes

This is a simple game that is easy to explain and fun for your young players. As such, it's perfect for your first practice.

This drill offers great "stopping the ball" repetition.

Drill 3: Follow the Leader

Goal: Dribbling under control, cutting, and stopping the ball with the head up.

Suggested Story Line: You and your players are *explorers* headed deep into the *rain forest*. Look out! There may be pythons and jaguars and who-knows-what around every bend! Be careful! Follow the player in front of you closely so you don't get lost! (When addressing your players, use a name for this drill based on your story line; for example, spoken with a spooky voice: "Deeeeeeep into the Rain Forest!")

Setup: Rectangular practice grid and beyond (22 disc cones).

How to Run the Drill

Begin in the grid with your players lined up behind you with their soccer balls at their feet. Lead your players anywhere around the playing field and nearby environs. If you're comfortable dribbling a soccer ball, do so. If not, simply walk or jog at the front of your line of players, who will dribble their soccer balls behind you.

Use natural obstacles as much as possible. Lead your players around bushes, beneath bleachers, and through playground equipment. Build on your story line by having them "Duck!" under slithering pythons (low-hanging branches) and "Jump!" over lines of army ants (sticks). Have them "Hurry up!" when they're being stalked by an imaginary jaguar, and have

Grace, Ellie, Emily, and Olivia play Follow the Leader.

Follow the Leader

them "Stop!" (with one foot on the ball) when you're confronted by an angry wild pig with razor-sharp tusks, or when you come across a secret, overgrown temple deep in the jungle. Encourage them to control the ball at all times. Do plenty of twisting and turning so your players are required to cut the ball over and over.

After a few minutes, allow your players to take turns as leader. Let them embellish the story line as well.

Notes

This drill is great because it requires your players to dribble, cut, and stop the ball while keeping their heads up to see where you're taking them next.

Be sure you keep your players in "explorer mode" throughout the drill so they don't grow bored or restless.

Lead your players at a speed that keeps the drill challenging but not frustrating.

Use the time when other players are leading to offer praise and suggestions regarding your players' dribbling, cutting, and ball-stopping techniques.

Variation

After a few practices, team your players with a partner and have them follow each other around 1-on-1 while remaining inside the practice grid. In this variation, the game picks up speed and becomes almost a game of chase while, at the same time, the two-player teams must avoid running into one another. Your players will love it. You will, too, because the 1-on-1 variation forces your players to raise their skills a notch in order to keep up with each other.

For this variation, be sure you team less-advanced players with less-advanced players and more-advanced players with more-advanced players.

Drill 4: Switch

Goal: Dribbling under control and accelerating to a free ball—"getting to the ball first."

Suggested Story Line: Every player is about to get a new ball. The catch is that they have to leave their old ball behind—and get to any other player's ball as fast as they can the instant you yell "Switch!" But they'd better beware because there's a burglar in the house!

Switch!
Requires 22 disc cones to make a regular grid

Switch

Tell your players the burglar—that's you—will be moving among them, and that they'll have to take care of their balls (keep them under control) so you can't steal (kick) them away. (Don't actually kick your players' balls away; only threaten to do so. And be sure to keep your burglar antics *fun*, not *scary*.)

Setup: Rectangular practice grid (22 disc cones).

How to Run the Drill

Essentially this drill is "musical soccer balls." The key idea of the drill is for players to learn to be fastest to the ball.

Have your players begin dribbling their balls around inside the grid. Tell them they must control their balls and stay away from you, the burglar.

Jog after your players making sneaky, burglar-like sounds. Your players will love trying to stay away from you. In doing so, they'll have to dribble and cut and stop their balls constantly.

Call out "Switch!" and encourage your players to leave their balls and switch to unoccupied balls as quickly as possible. Tell them to hurry and beat the burglar to their new balls.

Notes

In addition to requiring players to dribble, cut, and stop the ball, this drill introduces young players to the concept of getting to a free ball first.

The idea of *charging to* a ball is a surprisingly difficult concept for many 7-and-above youth soccer players to grasp. Many tend to wait for a rolling ball to come to them rather than running to it. As a result, the ball often is taken away before it reaches them by opposing players who understand the concept of getting to the ball first (perhaps because they played lots of Switch as 6-and-under players).

Drill 5: Alligator Pit

Goal: Dribbling under control, cutting the ball, and avoiding obstacles.
Suggested Story Line: Watch out for the giant alligators—*and* the evil swamp monster!
Setup: Rectangular practice grid (22 disc cones) with at least 10 upright cones set randomly throughout.

How to Run the Drill

Have your players begin dribbling around the grid in the same direction. Shout, "Cross the pit!" At that point, your players are to cut the ball into the grid or "pit," and dribble across it, cutting the ball as necessary to avoid the cone "alligators" lurking in the swamp. Add excitement to the drill by acting as a swamp monster while your players cross the pit. Charge at them growling and flashing your fingers as claws. They'll love trying to avoid you as they dribble.

Have your players switch the direction they're dribbling around the grid every couple of minutes.

Requires 22 disc cones to make a regular grid, plus at least 10 upright cones for the alligators
Cross the pit!

Alligator Pit

Notes

This drill really encourages your players to cut, or turn, the ball. Changing the direction they dribble around the grid is especially effective because, depending on their direction of travel, your players are required to cut the ball alternately with their right and left feet as they turn to race across the pit.

Your acting as a swamp monster enables you to increase the drill's level of difficulty for your more coordinated players by approaching them as a monster more often or more quickly than you approach your less coordinated players. Don't kick your players' balls away from them—that will come later, when your players are ready for it, with Crab Soccer and with Sharks and Minnows. Be sure you tone down your monster's scariness for your more timid players.

Drill 6: Trash Day

Goal: Moving to, turning, dribbling, and shooting the ball.
Suggested Story Line: Yippee! Your players get to be litterbugs! The neighbors are "throwing trash" (kicking soccer balls) into their yard. It's up to them to "throw" (kick) the trash over the "fence" (line of cones) and back into their neighbors' yard.
Setup: Rectangular practice grid (22 disc cones) divided width-wise into two "yards" by a line of 4 upright cones.

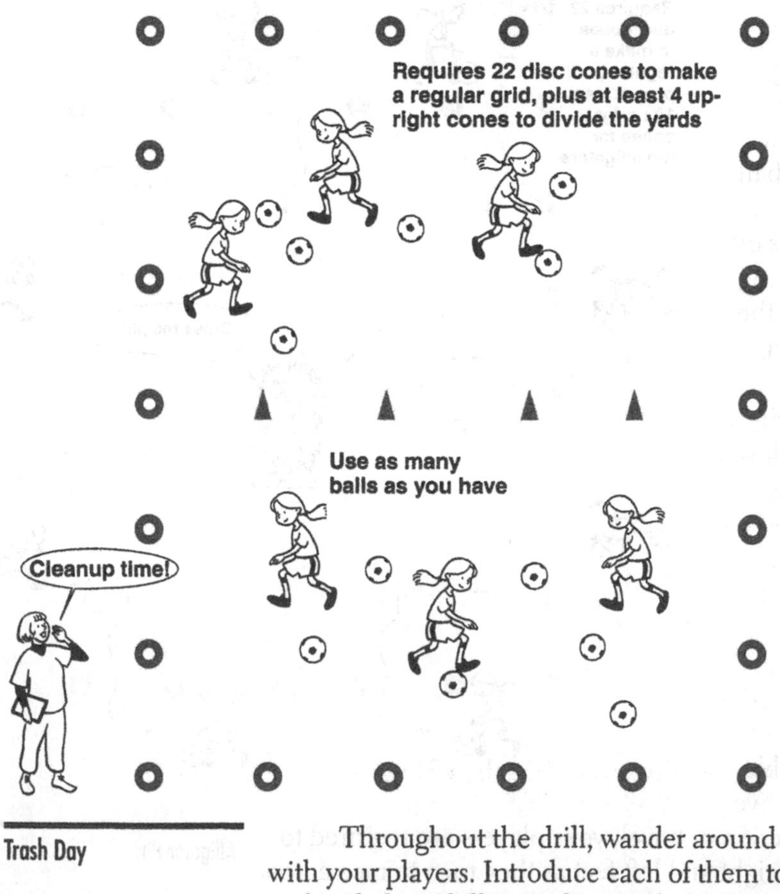

Requires 22 disc cones to make a regular grid, plus at least 4 upright cones to divide the yards

Use as many balls as you have

Cleanup time!

Trash Day

How to Run the Drill

Divide players into two squads and have one squad stand in each "yard."

Toss as many balls as are available into both yards and have your players begin booting the balls into each other's yards. Your players may dribble up to the line of cones and kick each ball from there, or they may simply kick each ball from wherever it is lying in the yard.

After a few minutes, have your players switch yards (simply as a change of pace), and then restart the drill.

Encourage your players to get rid of the trash by really sinking their feet into their shots. Encourage them, as well, to run to each ball.

Throughout the drill, wander around the grid working individually with your players. Introduce each of them to the correct shooting technique, as detailed in Skill 7: Kicking with the Instep, or Shooting, on pages 99–101.

Offer lots of encouragement and very little in the way of criticism. Remember, shooting is a complex and advanced skill. You're just taking advantage of the potential offered by this particular drill to give your players a taste of it.

Have your players hustle after balls in their yards (their halves of the grid) and any that have gone out of their yards—there will be many. Have your players dribble balls back into their yards before shooting.

Notes

Trash Day provides a tremendous opportunity to teach your players to kick with the instep (and *not* with the toes—before they ever pick up that bad habit).

Skill 7: Kicking with the Instep, or Shooting

Your players want to score goals. For now they'll be able to do so simply by dribbling the ball into the goal. Soon enough, however, they'll be required to shoot to score goals, and they'll need to know the proper way to shoot.

How to Shoot the Ball

1. Step into the ball. Without prompting, many players will at first try to shoot the ball by standing with the ball at their feet and simply swinging the kicking leg at it. Of course, they won't generate much power on their shots when they do so.

   Instead, a player should stand a few paces behind the ball and approach the ball at an angle and at a slow jog. She should plant her nonkicking foot (usually the left foot to begin with, as most soccer players are naturally right-footed) alongside the ball so that her toes are roughly in line with the center of the ball and her planted leg is slightly bent at the knee.

   Note that the planted foot is the target foot. Wherever it points is where the ball is going. (This information is provided for your information only. It won't become important to your players until they're older.)
2. Swing the kicking leg. Many young players will try to kick the ball with a straight leg. However, the kicking foot should swing back until the heel nearly touches the buttocks—that is, the knee should be fully bent.

   The toes should be pointed all the way through the shot so as to strike the ball with the widest part of the foot—the laces. The ankle should remain locked to give the shot its power.
3. Keep the head down through the shot. Many young players look up to see where their kicks are going before they complete their kicks. This results in errant or weak kicks.

   Players should look at the ball by keeping their head down and over the ball throughout each shot.
4. Land on the kicking leg. After their shots, players should follow through

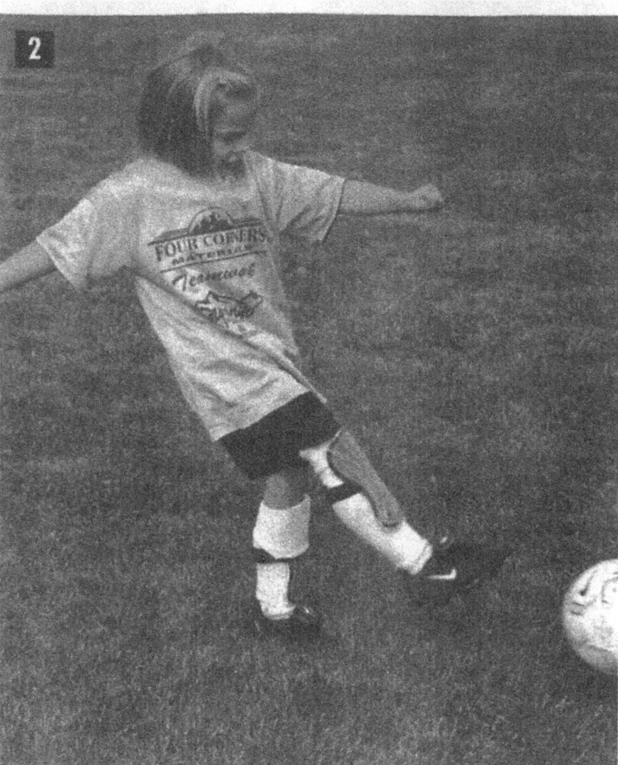

Olivia points her toes down to shoot with her instep. (1)

Olivia follows through after her shot for maximum power. (2)

and land on the kicking foot. This follow-through gives their shots maximum power.

Players should not jump into the air as they shoot. Rather, the momentum of kicking the ball should simply propel them forward so that they wind up, effectively, taking a big step.

Young players who do not land on the kicking foot are instead leaning backward and removing much of the power from their shots as they kick the ball.

How to Teach Shooting

Don't worry about the four-part technical description above when it comes to introducing your young players to shooting a soccer ball. The description is provided for your benefit only, so that you'll know where you'll eventually take your players.

For now, at the 6-and-under level, each time you run Trash Day with your players, simply tell them to come at the ball and boot it hard with their laces. Then spend your time encouraging your players to indeed kick the ball with their laces as opposed to with their toes. Just doing that will keep you plenty busy.

If you have time, you might talk with some of your players about keeping their head down and following through with their shots as opposed to leaning backward.

Shooting

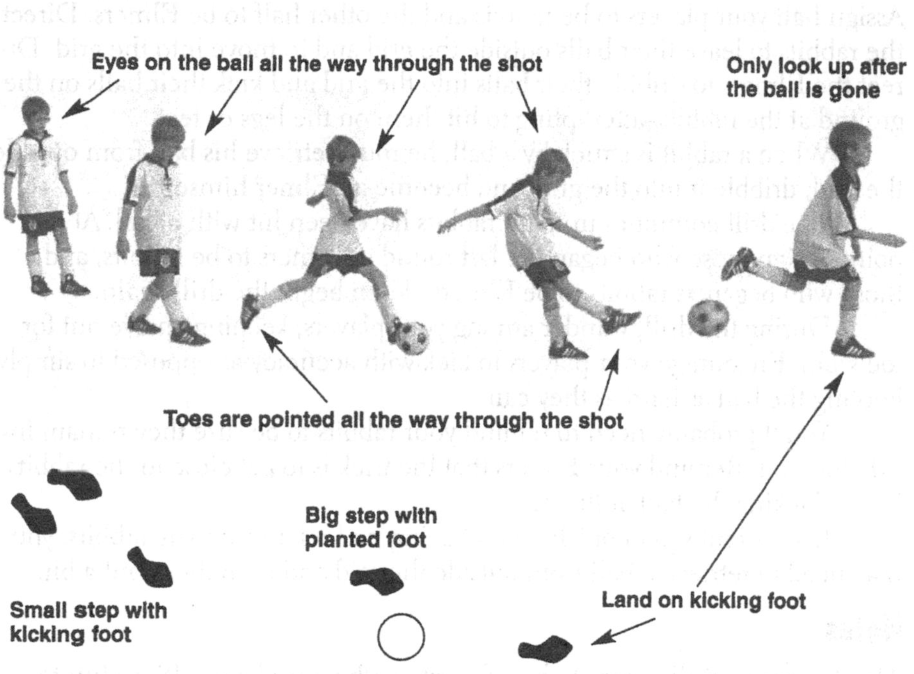
Eyes on the ball all the way through the shot
Only look up after the ball is gone
Toes are pointed all the way through the shot
Big step with planted foot
Small step with kicking foot
Land on kicking foot

Drill 7: Elmer Fudd

Drill 7: Elmer Fudd

Goal: Dribbling under control and shooting or passing at a moving target.

Suggested Story Line: You'll likely find that most of your young players—not schooled in Bugs Bunny lore—will be prone to call this drill Elmer "Fudge" as opposed to Elmer Fudd. It'll be up to you to tell them the story of Elmer and the wily Bugs Bunny, of how quickly Bugs Bunny moves, and of how accurate the Elmers must be with their shots in order to hit the fast bunnies.

Setup: Rectangular practice grid (22 disc cones).

Elmer Fudd

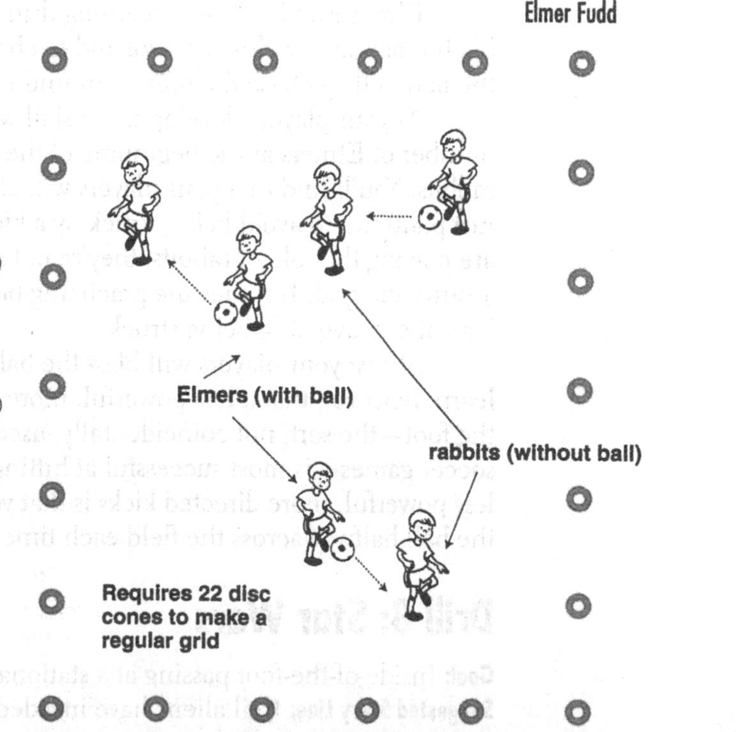
Elmers (with ball)
rabbits (without ball)
Requires 22 disc cones to make a regular grid

How to Run the Drill

Assign half your players to be rabbits and the other half to be Elmers. Direct the rabbits to leave their balls outside the grid and to move into the grid. Direct the Elmers to dribble their balls into the grid and kick their balls on the ground at the rabbits, attempting to hit them on the legs or feet.

When a rabbit is struck by a ball, he must retrieve his ball from outside the grid, dribble it into the grid, and become an Elmer himself.

The drill continues until all rabbits have been hit with a ball. At that point, assign those who began the last round as Elmers to be rabbits, and those who began as rabbits to be Elmers. Then begin the drill again.

During the drill, wander among your players, keeping an eye out for toe kicks. Encourage your players to kick with accuracy as opposed to simply booting the ball as hard as they can.

You'll probably need to remind your rabbits to be sure they remain inside the grid. Remind your Elmers that the trick is to get close to the rabbits before kicking the ball at them.

If a current squad of Elmers is having no luck hitting any rabbits, you may need to retrieve a ball from outside the grid and help them out a bit.

Notes

This fast-paced drill is sure to be a favorite with your players. It's so fun to play, in fact, that we often wind up playing it along with our players rather than doing the coaching as we should be doing.

Elmer Fudd is a great learning drill because it requires players to dribble the ball under close control and to change direction quickly by cutting the ball as they chase the rabbits around the grid.

As your players develop more skill with the ball, you may reduce the number of Elmers at the beginning of the game and increase the number of rabbits. You'll find that your players will clamor to be rabbits; the fact is, it's just plain fun to avoid being struck by a kicked ball. Of course, while players are playing the role of rabbits, they're not actively kicking and moving a ball around the grid. But they *are* practicing body movement and control as they leap about, avoiding being struck.

At first your players will blast the ball at the rabbits. They'll quickly learn, however, that a less powerful, more directed kick using the inside of the foot—the sort, not coincidentally, used most often to pass the ball during soccer games—is most successful at hitting rabbits. An added incentive of less powerful, more directed kicks is that your players won't have to chase the ball halfway across the field each time they shoot and miss.

Drill 8: Star Wars

Goal: Inside-of-the-foot passing at a stationary target.
Suggested Story Line: Evil aliens have invaded our "solar system" (the grid). It's

up to your players to "knock out their spaceships" (knock over the upright cones in the grid) before the aliens invade our planet!

Setup: Rectangular practice grid (22 disc cones) with at least 10 cones set randomly throughout.

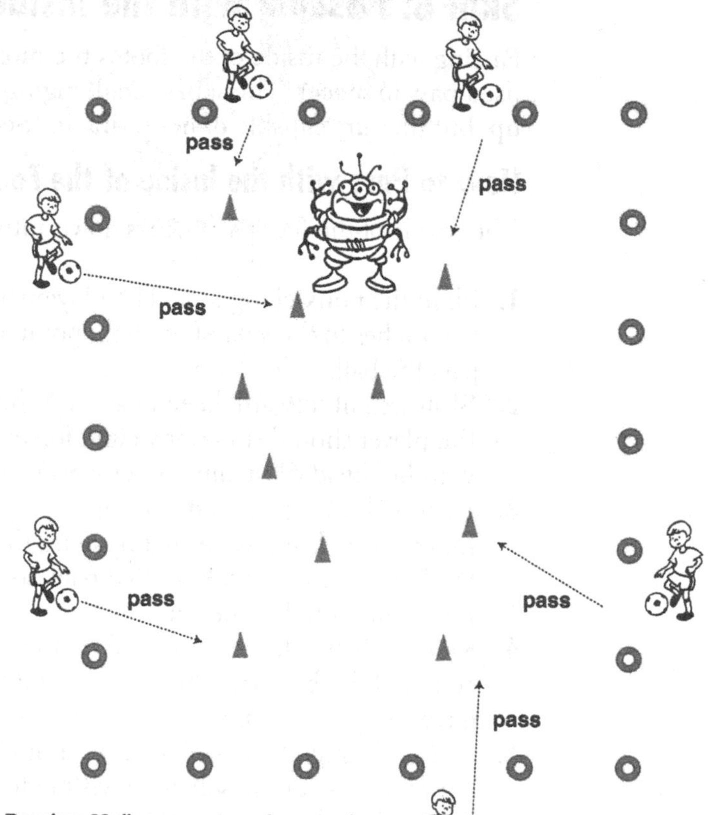

pass

pass

pass

pass

pass

pass

Requires 22 disc cones to make a regular grid, plus at least 10 upright cones for the spaceships

How to Run the Drill

Start with your players, each with a ball at their feet, spread along the outside of the grid. Have them begin "shooting" (kicking) their ball at the "spaceships" (cones) in the middle of the grid using inside-of-the-foot passes. (See Skill 8: Passing with the Inside of the Foot on pages 104–6.)

Direct players to retrieve their own ball and continue shooting from outside the square. Have them set up any cones they manage to knock down.

If you wish, you may let your players keep score. Be sure to only add up the number of spaceships they zap—that is, the number of cones they knock over—as a team rather than keeping individual scores.

Add excitement to the drill by becoming an alien yourself and zooming near your players as they attempt their kicks. In particular, zoom menacingly close to your more advanced players to make the drill more challenging for them.

Star Wars

Notes

Make sure your players are "shooting" at the spaceships using inside-of-the-foot passes.

As with Alligator Pit, don't kick your players' balls away from them when you threaten them as an alien. That will come with Crab Soccer and with Sharks and Minnows.

Offer much encouragement and little, if any, criticism of your players as they attempt to pass the ball with the inside of the foot. As with shooting, passing with the inside of the foot is an advanced soccer skill. You're simply introducing it to your players at this point.

Skill 8: Passing with the Inside of the Foot

Passing with the inside of the foot is the most accurate and most frequently used pass in soccer. The skill is challenging for 6-and-under players to pick up, but they *are* capable of mastering it. (See photos opposite.)

How to Pass with the Inside of the Foot

The inside-of-the-foot pass breaks down into five steps:

1. Plant the nonkicking foot. The player should plant her nonkicking foot a few inches to the side of the ball, pointed in the direction she wishes to pass the ball.
2. Shift weight forward; keep head over the ball. As she initiates the pass, the player should shift her weight forward and onto her planted foot, with her head down and directly over the ball.
3. Position kicking foot out, toes up. The player should bring the kicking foot back with the knee slightly bent, the foot turned out from her body 90 degrees, and her toes pulled back so that her ankle is locked, with her heel down and her toes up.
4. Kick the ball with the inside of the foot. The player should strike the center of the ball with the inside of the foot. If hit correctly, the ball will have a slight topspin to it.
5. Follow through. The kicking foot should rise high enough off the ground after the kick for the sole to be visible to an onlooker standing in front of the passing player.

How to Teach Passing with the Inside of the Foot

The best way to teach your players the correct foot position for passing with the inside of the foot is to walk around like a duck and have your players mimic you. Swing both your feet out wide, raise your toes, and rock back on your heels. Now waddle around the field with your players as they do the same thing. Remember—and this is critical—quacking and wing flapping are mandatory.

As with shooting the ball, passing

Inside of Foot Pass

Head is over the ball
Plant nonkicking foot pointing at target

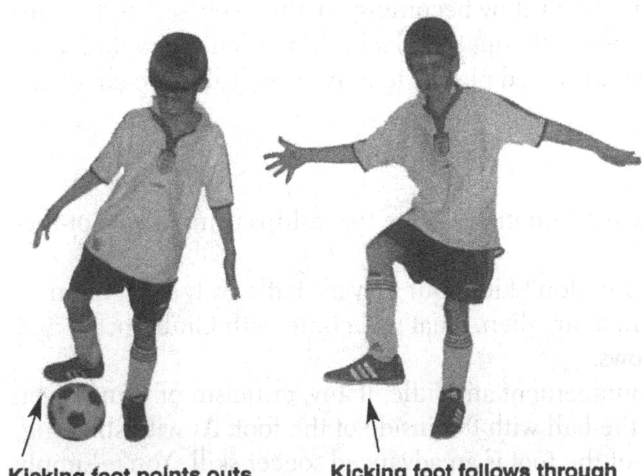
Kicking foot points outs with heel down and toes up
Kicking foot follows through

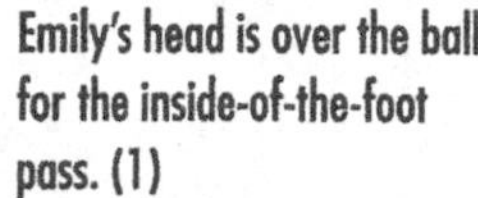

Emily's head is over the ball for the inside-of-the-foot pass. (1)

Emily's planted foot points where the ball will go. (2)

Emily's heel is down and her toes are up. (3)

The sole of Emily's cleat is visible when she follows through. (4)

with the inside of the foot is an advanced skill that you're simply introducing to your players through the Star Wars drill.

Don't worry much about whether your players manage all five steps of the inside-of-the-foot pass at this point. Simply encourage them to use the insides of their feet, with their toes up and their heels down, to strike their soccer balls as they "shoot" at the "spaceships" in the grid.

Drill 9: Crab Soccer

Goal: Downfield dribbling while avoiding obstacles.
Suggested Story Line: This drill is so fun it doesn't need much in the way of a story line. You'll need to tell your players only that the giant crabs are out, and that they'd better be careful!

Setup: Rectangular practice grid (22 disc cones).

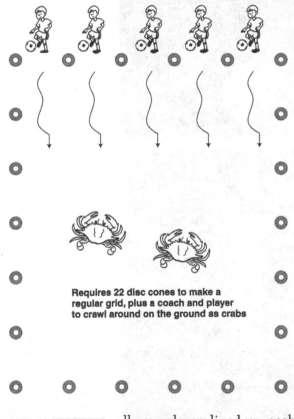

Requires 22 disc cones to make a regular grid, plus a coach and player to crawl around on the ground as crabs

Crab Soccer

How to Run the Drill

Each player starts with a ball on one end of the grid while you assume the position and role of a giant crab in the middle of the grid. Assume the crab position by raising yourself from the ground on your hands and feet while facing up. (See photo.)

On your command, have your players dribble their balls from one end of the grid to the other while you attempt to kick any of their balls out of the grid. Players whose balls you manage to kick out or who accidentally kick their balls out of the grid themselves then join you as crabs, after which the remaining players attempt to dribble back up the length of the grid, again at your command, this time past you and any new crabs.

The drill continues until everyone has become a crab, after which you'll run it again by starting out as the sole crab with all your players lined up, each behind a ball, at one end of the grid.

Remind and encourage players to remain inside the grid as they dribble from one end of the grid to the other.

Notes

Be sure to encourage your players to dribble the ball under control. Some players will try to kick the ball the entire length of the grid and then run af-

Olivia dribbles through the crabs.

ter it. This isn't good soccer, nor is it safe, as it can result in a "crab" getting hurt by being struck in the face by a ball.

As specified in the following chapter, we offer this drill for the first time as part of the final practice session for 4- and 5-year-old players. Crab soccer represents the first real taste of dribbling under pressure such young players will experience during practice.

Most very young players will be ready to try dribbling under pressure by their sixth practice and will relish the added challenge of doing so. Some, however, may not be ready. If that's the case with any of your players, don't push them. Allow any who wish to sit out to do so during this drill. If the majority of your players aren't quite ready for Crab Soccer, wait a couple of weeks, or even until next season, before you try it again.

Drill 10: Sharks and Minnows

Goal: Practicing acceleration while dribbling under control.
Suggested Story Line: This drill essentially is Crab Soccer with speed—a quicker, more competitive version of the game wherein the "crabs," who were crawling around on all fours, have become "sharks," who run around on their feet. That's why you'll run it as part of the practice sessions in the following chapter for teams of 5- and 6-year-olds as opposed to teams of 4- and 5-year-olds.

Most 5- and 6-year-old soccer players love Sharks and Minnows. No real storytelling is necessary to hold their attention while they play it. The first time you run the drill, you'll need to simply line up your players and get the drill going. After you've run Sharks and Minnows once, each time you announce to your players, "It's time for Sharks and Minnows!" you'll be met with an excited cheer.
Setup: Rectangular practice grid (22 disc cones).

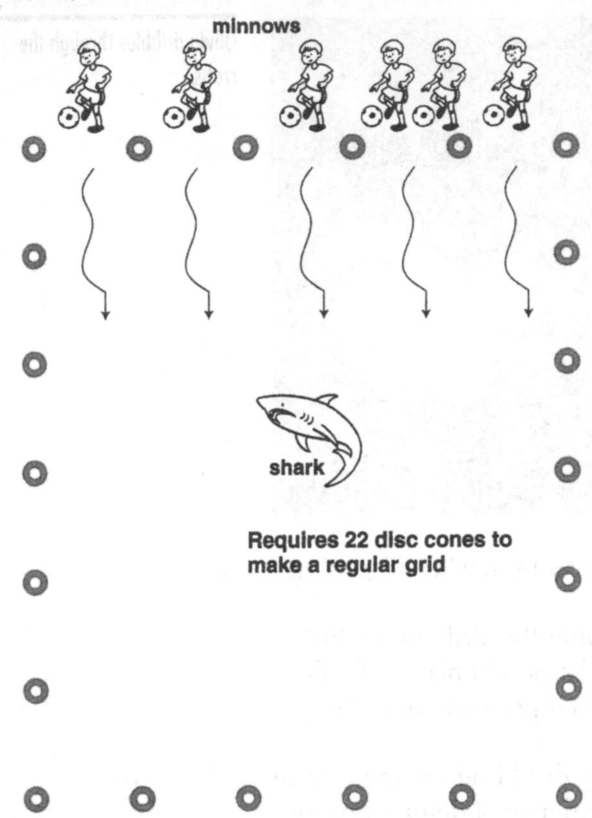
minnows
shark
Requires 22 disc cones to make a regular grid

Sharks and Minnows

How to Run the Drill

Each player starts with a ball at one end of the grid while you assume the position and role of a fearsome shark standing in the middle of the grid.

On your command, have your players dribble their balls from one end of the grid to the other while you run at them and attempt to kick any of their balls out of the grid. Players whose balls you manage to kick out or who accidentally kick their balls out of the grid themselves then join you as sharks, after which the remaining players attempt to dribble back up the length of the grid, again at your command, this time past you and any new sharks.

The drill continues until the last minnow has been caught, after which you'll run it again by starting out as the sole shark, with all your players again lined up with their balls at one end of the grid as minnows.

As with Crab Soccer, remind and encourage minnows to remain within the grid as they dribble from one end of it to the other.

Notes

This drill is great because it teaches players to *accelerate* with the ball while keeping the ball under control, just as they must in game situations. At your command, your players will begin dribbling down the grid. Then, when they see an opening, they'll accelerate and dribble down the grid at top speed, attempting to get to the other end of the grid before you can reach them and kick their balls out of the grid.

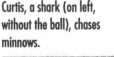

Curtis, a shark (on left, without the ball), chases minnows.

You'll help your players best learn how to accelerate while keeping the ball under control by zeroing in on those players who boot their soccer balls far ahead before chasing after them. Those balls provide easy pickings for you as a shark. Once you've picked those balls off a few times, the players who kicked them will get the idea that they must accelerate while not kicking the ball so far out in front of them—just as they must during games.

It's possible that some of your players will start out feeling a bit uncomfortable with the competitive nature of this drill. Feel free to allow them to sit out the drill at first, or to join you as a shark at the beginning of each round of the drill until they're ready to join in as minnows.

Many of your players will enjoy playing the role of sharks as much as or more than they'll enjoy being minnows. Feel free to allow your players to take turns in your place as the beginning shark. Moreover, don't worry too much about those minnows who allow sharks to kick their balls out of the grid so they quickly can become sharks themselves. Because of the attacking and ball-tackling skills required of sharks, the role of shark during Sharks and Minnows is as great a learning and playing opportunity as the role of minnow.

Drill 11: Steal the Bacon

Goal: Dribbling under control with the intent of scoring, as well as receiving with the inside of the foot.

Suggested Story Line: This drill creates its own game-like stories and scenarios as players learn to compete against one another in 1-on-1 and 2-on-2 situations.

Setup: Modified rectangular practice grid (18 disc cones) with pairs of cones (4 cones) 4 yards (or four paces) apart at each end as goals.

How to Run the Drill

Divide your players into two squads. Name each player in one squad as a fierce or fast animal and each player in the other squad as one of the same animals. With two squads of three players, you'll then have, say, two tigers, two lions, and two cheetahs. Be *absolutely sure* to match players by animal according to their levels of ability and aggressiveness as best you can.

We suggest you avoid assigning your players using numbers because your players will remember their assigned animal types better than they will numbers. Also, numbers invariably tend to suggest a ranking of ability, something always worth avoiding—even though, in fact, you will be pairing players based on ability.

Send each squad to an opposite corner of the grid and have them sit down there, just

Steal the Bacon

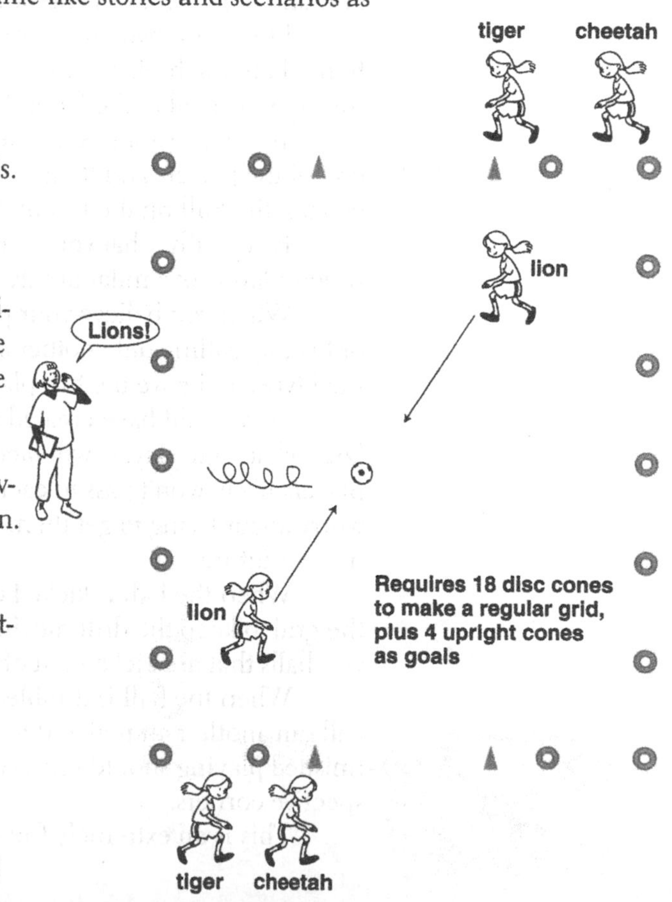
tiger
cheetah
lion
Lions!
lion
Requires 18 disc cones to make a regular grid, plus 4 upright cones as goals
tiger
cheetah

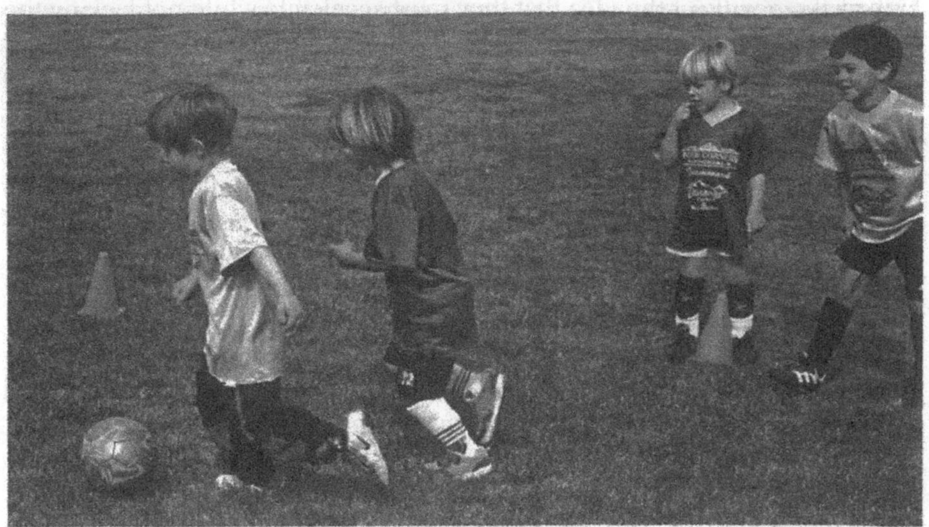

Leo and George play Steal the Bacon.

outside the grid. Quickly, before they grow restless, call out one of the three animal names. At the same time, roll a ball into the middle of the grid.

Direct the two players of the animal type you've just called out to run to the ball. Each player tries to gain control of the ball and dribble it through the goal at the far end of the grid from where she was just seated.

You may want to start the drill by rolling the ball in the direction of one of the players and then use the opportunity to run through Skill 9: Receiving the Ball on the Ground, which is detailed on page 112.

Essentially what you're doing is setting up a 1-on-1 scrimmage between players of similar ability and aggressiveness.

When you believe your players are ready for it, probably after a practice or two, try calling out another animal type shortly after calling out the first animal type, and have the two players with the second assigned animal join in.

Now you'll have created a 2-on-2 scrimmage that more closely simulates what your players will face in game situations. Note that your young players likely won't pass to each other during 2-on-2 Steal the Bacon. Don't worry about trying to get them to do so. The whole concept of passing is still in their future.

When the ball is kicked out of the grid, simply toss another ball into the grid to keep the drill moving. Have waiting players fetch and return to you balls that are kicked out of the grid.

When the ball is dribbled or kicked through one of the goals, quickly call out another animal and toss another ball into the grid. Those who just finished playing should retrieve the ball, toss it to you, and return to their respective corners.

This is an extremely fun and active drill as long as you keep it moving.

Notes

This is the most competitive drill we suggest you run with your 6-and-under players. In the following chapter, we include it only in the practice sessions for older players.

When they're ready for it, your players will love Steal the Bacon—and will learn a great deal from it. If your players don't take to Steal the Bacon the first time you run it with them because it's a bit too competitive for them, don't push it. Wait a few practices, then try it again. Believe us, soon it will be their all-time favorite drill.

This is a great drill for the end of practice. Your players will be tired and ready to sit and wait their turn during the drill.

No matter how hard you try, you won't be able to match all your players perfectly by ability and aggressiveness. In response to this reality, you can—and should—help weaker players by tossing the ball directly to them when you call their animals so that they begin with the ball in their control.

Your aim, as coach, should be to make each paired match as even as possible because that's when your players will have the most fun—and thus learn the most soccer.

Strongly encourage your players to control the ball and attempt to dribble around one another; they should dribble all the way through the goal during this drill rather than taking long shots at the goal.

(By instinct, most 6-and-under players want to kick the ball as hard as they can. During games, many parents will encourage their children to do just that—despite the fact that big kicks simply result in giving possession of the ball to the other team. Dribbling and ball control are what soccer is all about. When, under your direction, your players learn to dribble rather than take big kicks during Steal the Bacon, they'll naturally begin to play the same way during games.)

Calling out all three animals to create a 3-on-3 scrimmage doesn't work well in the small confines of the practice grid. We recommend you stick with 1-on-1 and 2-on-2 scrimmages for Steal the Bacon and leave the confusion and swarm style of play that invariably results from 3-on-3 scrimmages for game day.

That said, calling out all three animal types at once as you toss the ball into the grid makes a great, chaotic, fun way to conclude this drill, one that will leave your players happy and breathless with excitement.

Variation

Eventually, try setting up some 1-on-2 situations for your players. This will require one player to attempt to dribble past two players to advance the ball up the grid. Conversely, the two-player team might actually pass the ball back and forth to one another as they attempt to advance the ball up the grid against their single defender—but don't hold your breath.

Skill 9: Receiving the Ball on the Ground

Steal the Bacon provides you the opportunity to introduce the receiving-the-ball-on-the-ground skill to your players. Introducing this skill also will help your players learn not to charge to the ball and kick it with all their might when their animal type is called—one of the hazards of this drill. Instead, you can use the introduction of this skill to encourage your players to receive the ball correctly and then to set off dribbling it.

How to Receive the Ball

The simplest and surest way for a player to receive a ball that is rolling on the ground is with the inside of the foot.

As the ball approaches, the player should lift her receiving foot slightly off the ground so the middle of the ball strikes the inside of the foot. The foot position is the same as for the inside-of-the-foot pass: the heel is down, the toes are up, and the foot is at 90 degrees to the rolling ball. The player should cushion the ball as it strikes her foot so that the ball bounces off her foot and rolls in front of her body, ready to be dribbled or, when she's older, passed.

Receiving a Rolling Ball

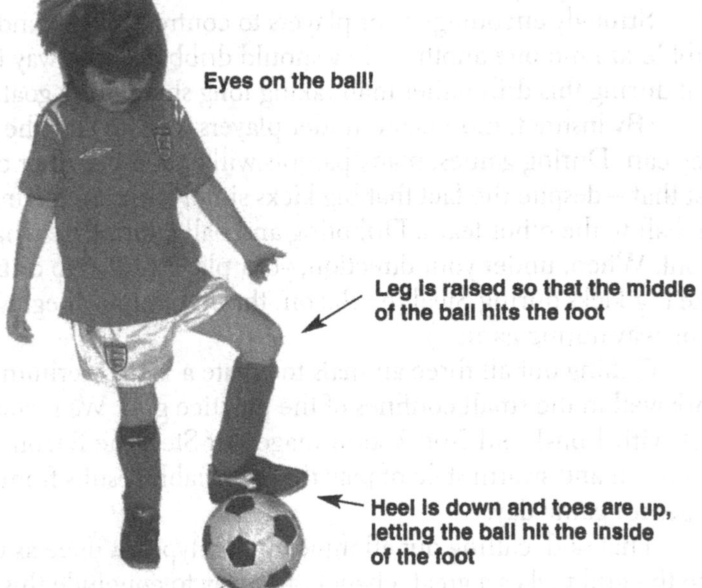
Eyes on the ball!
Leg is raised so that the middle of the ball hits the foot
Heel is down and toes are up, letting the ball hit the inside of the foot

How to Teach Receiving the Ball

Every now and then when initiating a round of Steal the Bacon, roll the ball in the direction of one player instead of into the middle of the grid. This will allow the player to receive the ball without pressure from his opponent.

Halt the drill for a moment to praise what the player did correctly when he attempted to receive the ball, and offer a suggestion for improvement based on the technical description above. Then quickly get the drill moving again.

Drill 12: Freeze Tag

Goal: Dribbling in all directions under control, and shielding, or protecting, the ball.
Suggested Story Line: Warn your players there's a big bad Ice Age coming, and that they'd better keep moving, and keep their soccer balls well protected, if they don't want to end up—Aaaack!—frozen solid!
Setup: Rectangular practice grid (22 disc cones).

How to Run the Drill

Designate one player as the "*Freeeeeeeze*master." Have the rest of your players begin dribbling around inside the grid. Release the Freezemaster into the grid to attempt to steal the dribblers' balls and kick them out of the grid.

When a player's ball is kicked out of the grid, he must retrieve it, run back inside the grid with it, and stand with it atop his head and with his legs spread (see photos next page). When another player dribbles the ball through the frozen player's legs, he becomes unfrozen, puts the ball down, and begins dribbling around inside the grid again.

If your designated Freezemaster is having difficulty freezing everyone, help her out by becoming Freezemaster yourself or by designating a second player to become a Freezemaster.

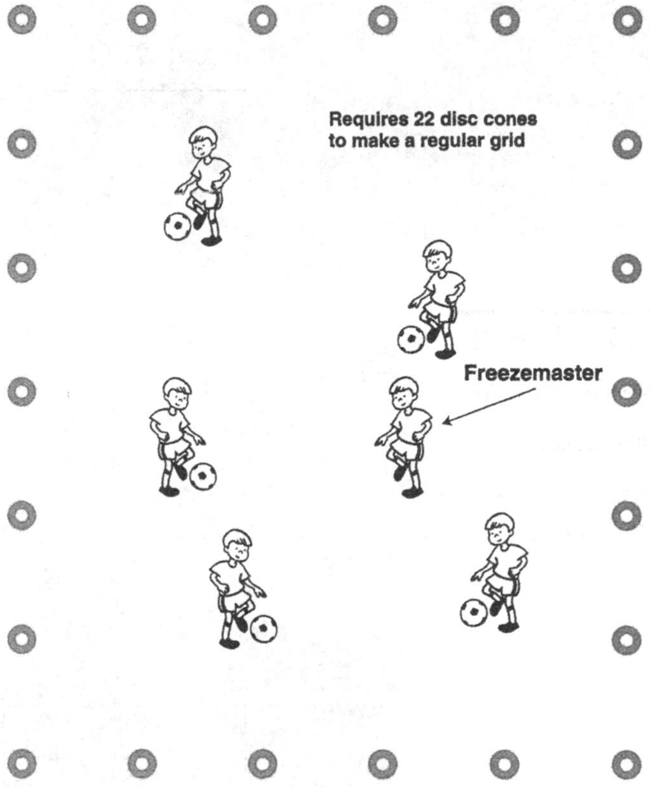

The round ends when all players are frozen. At that point, designate another Freezemaster and start another round.

Requires 22 disc cones
to make a regular grid
Freezemaster

Freeze Tag

Notes

To really get your players dribbling and shielding the ball, feel free to designate yourself as the Freezemaster and move up the level of play accordingly.

Offer praise and one suggestion for improvement per player regarding your players' efforts at shielding the ball (see Skill 10: Shielding the Ball on pages 115–16) on an individual basis while the drill continues around you and the player you're working with.

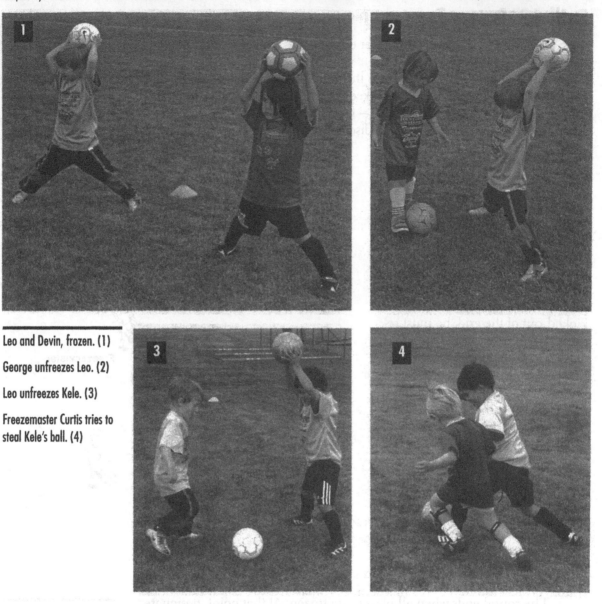

Leo and Devin, frozen. (1)

George unfreezes Leo. (2)

Leo unfreezes Kele. (3)

Freezemaster Curtis tries to steal Kele's ball. (4)

Variation

Once you've covered the juggling skill in practice, challenge players whose balls are kicked out of the grid to complete a successful juggle—drop, kick, and catch—of the ball as their way of unfreezing themselves and reentering the game as opposed to merely standing in the middle of the grid with their legs spread, waiting to be unfrozen.

Skill 10: Shielding the Ball

A player can maintain possession and make it very difficult for an opponent to steal the ball by using his body as a shield between his opponent and the ball. Your players will naturally use their bodies as shields while they play Freeze Tag. As a result, the drill provides a great opportunity for you to introduce to your players the correct way to perform this advanced skill.

How to Shield the Ball

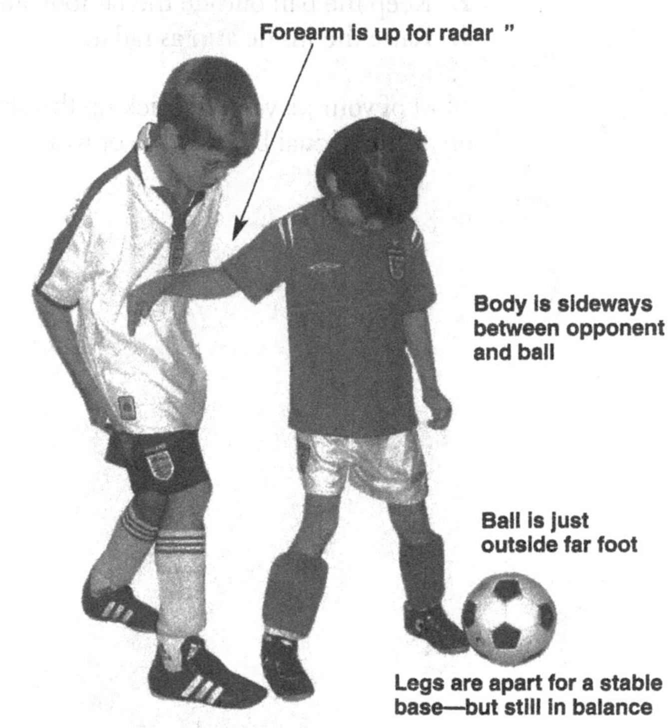
Forearm is up for radar "
Body is sideways between opponent and ball
Ball is just outside far foot
Legs are apart for a stable base—but still in balance

A player shields the ball by placing her body between the ball and her opponent because in soccer a foul is committed when a defensive player "goes through" an offensive player to get the ball. If a player maneuvers her body effectively, an opponent cannot get to the ball without fouling.

The most effective way to shield the ball from an opponent is for a player to turn her body sideways between her opponent and the ball so that the ball is just outside her far foot.

The player's legs should be spread about shoulder width apart to establish a wide but balanced base. This position makes it nearly impossible for an opponent to reach a leg in and kick the ball away.

Shielding

As the opponent moves around the player to get at the ball, the player simply pivots around the ball in response. (Smart players wait for the opponent to commit to coming around them in one direction, then quickly dribble the ball away in the other direction.)

A player may use "radar" to help shield the ball. She raises the forearm nearest her opponent to maintain a bit of distance between herself and her opponent and to act as an early-warning radar that senses when her opponent leans in harder, stepping up the attack. Use of the arm as a radar is legal in soccer, but pushing off with the arm is not.

How to Teach Shielding

The best way to introduce shielding to your players is on a one-on-one basis during the game of Freeze Tag. Simply visit with one of your players for a moment, demonstrating the correct sideways technique for shielding the ball, and then step back and encourage the player to have a go at it when the Freezemaster approaches.

Encourage each of your players to:

1. Remain sideways to the Freezemaster;
2. Keep the ball outside the far foot; and
3. Raise the inside arm as radar.

Most of your players will pick up this skill after you demonstrate it to them on an individual basis a time or two.

Your First Six Practices

Quick Coaching Guide

Every possible minute of every practice, concentrate on enabling *all* your players to touch and move the ball with their feet as much as possible.

Your players will appreciate the highly structured practice sessions you'll run with them, as detailed in this chapter.

Spend your limited practice time with your players, teaching and learning through fun drills as opposed to holding team scrimmages.

If you're a creative, fun-loving, storytelling coach, your players will love playing with you.

Soccer *is* ball movement and ball control.

Every other soccer skill is less important at this age. That's why your job as a coach of young players is so simple. As a coach, you need to concentrate only on enabling your 6-and-under players to touch and move the ball with their feet as much as possible—a theoretical thousand times each practice. The time and place you need to do this is during your team's all-important practice sessions.

This chapter includes two sets of minute-by-minute practice sessions that emphasize ball movement and control over all other aspects of the game of soccer. The sessions are presented in easy-to-photocopy format so that you may copy and attach them to your clipboard or stick them in your pocket for use during practice.

> **"Soccer is ball movement and ball control. Every other soccer skill is less important at this age."**

Each practice session includes the introduction of a basic ball-control skill as detailed in Chapter 8, Basic Ball-Control Skills and the Red Light/Green Light Drill. You'll introduce the skills in order so that they build on one another. The sets of practice sessions are divided by age—one set of practices for coaching 4- and 5-year-olds, and a second set of practices offering slightly more advanced drills for coaching 5- and 6-year-olds.

Highly Structured

Note that the practice sessions are highly structured. Children age 6 and under crave structure. The predictable nature of the practice sessions you'll run will answer this craving. As a result, your players will relax and have fun within the set routine you'll take them through in every practice.

Each practice is broken into 10-minute blocks. Practices for 4- and 5-year-olds are 40 minutes long. Those for 5- and 6-year-olds are 60 minutes long.

You'll take a quick water break with your team every 20 minutes. Keep the breaks short by encouraging your players to jog over to their water bottles, drink from them while standing up, and jog back to the practice grids. (You may even want to have your players station their water bottles close at hand between your two practice grids.)

The first two 10-minute blocks of each practice are devoted to learning and practicing basic ball-control skills by playing Drill 1: Red Light/Green Light (see page 67). The remaining 10-minute blocks of each practice are

Scrimmages? What Scrimmages?

We don't offer any time for intrasquad scrimmages during the practice sessions we present in this chapter. That's because scrimmages do not teach young players the game of soccer.

Essentially, 6-and-under scrimmages are for the team's most coordinated player. That player will largely control the ball, and thus the scrimmage, while the rest of the members of the team chase around after her. As such, scrimmages tend to further widen the ability gap between the most advanced player and the rest of the players on the team.

As it is, the less advanced players on your team will spend lots of time chasing ineffectually after the ball during your team's official games. There's no need to compound that problem by running scrimmages during your practices.

In fact, the best way to hold "scrimmages" with your team is to think of your weekly games as scrimmages. As long as you sufficiently de-emphasize the idea of winning and losing your official games—to yourself as well as to your players and parents—that line of thinking will work well.

Remember, the amount of time you have to practice with your team is limited. Your players will be better off if you dedicate that time to having *all* your players touch and move their own soccer balls with their feet as much as possible. Scrimmages won't accomplish that task, whereas the fun drills you'll run with your players during your practices will.

In the youth soccer world, it is said that lazy coaches scrimmage. Do your best not to be a lazy coach.

Keep in mind as well, however, that your players will enjoy scrimmaging against one another if you let them. If you're faced with a practice day when you're not feeling well or you don't have a parent helper to assist you, devoting part of a practice to an intrasquad scrimmage might just be in your and your players' best interests.

One final note: 6-and-under players tend to tell their coaches they want to scrimmage each other when they're bored with the drills that are being played during practice. If you keep the drills you run with your players fun and game-like enough, you won't face this problem.

Competition? What Competition?

Soccer's all about trying to take the ball away from the other guy. It's all about *competition*.

You know that. We know that. Everybody who's ever watched a soccer game knows that.

Even so, the practice sessions we present in this chapter for 6-and-under players emphasize having players touch and move the ball on their own, with little pressure or fear of losing the ball to someone else—that is, with virtually no hint of competition.

Why? For two reasons:

1. Children age 6 and under are not ready for the hard-core competitive aspects of game play that make competitive games fun for older kids and adults alike. Instead, young children learn by having fun.

Soon enough your players will love keeping score and fighting to win games. For now, however, the pressures associated with winning and losing games will do them more harm than good. If they feel that pressure, they will become fearful of losing, and they'll no longer enjoy playing soccer. And if they don't have fun playing soccer, they won't learn the game.

2. The only way to learn any new skill, whether you're an adult or a child, is in a noncompetitive environment.

Let's say you, as an adult, wanted to take up tennis for the first time. Would you take it up by entering a tournament? Of course not. You'd start by practicing, in a noncompetitive way, with someone else or on your own by hitting off a wall.

The same is true of soccer. The only way the youngsters on your team will learn to control the ball is by practicing basic ball-control skills over and over and over again in a noncompetitive environment. And the only way they'll practice those skills over and over is if you enable them to do so by following the practice sessions in this chapter that aim to make their practices fun, fun, fun.

As your players improve at the game of soccer, they naturally will begin looking for competitive ways to test their newly developed skills against one another during practice. That desire to test themselves probably will not occur among preschool-age players, but it likely will occur among those who are 5 and, more so, 6 years old. In response, you'll introduce the idea of true competition between your players during practice through Drill 11: Steal the Bacon, included in the set of practice sessions for 5- and 6-year-olds (see pages 109–11). Steal the Bacon provides the perfect entrée into the world of competition for your young players because you, as coach, directly control the drill's level of competitiveness.

devoted to playing fun drills with your team that reinforce the basic skills and introduce your players to the concepts of shooting, passing, receiving the ball on the ground, and shielding, as detailed in the preceding chapter.

After your first practice with your team, you'll introduce only *one* new drill and *one or two* new skills to your team for each of the next five practices. Before you leave home for each practice, be sure to read through and understand the drill and skill(s) you'll introduce to your players that particular practice.

Before Practice

As detailed in Chapter 5, On the Field, be sure to show up for your practices with the right attitude and equipment, ready to have fun with your young players.

Ball-Movement Skill Progression, as Presented in This Book

The practice sessions in this book encourage young players to attempt and learn skills in a logical and progressive manner.

First, your players will practice each skill *slowly and without pressure* during the Red Light/Green Light drill.

Next, your players will practice the skill *quickly and without pressure* during noncompetitive drills.

Then, your players will practice the skill *quickly and with pressure* during slightly competitive drills.

Finally, your players will use the skill *quickly and under pressure* during games and during Drill 11: Steal the Bacon.

Grid Size

Soccer coaching books for older players generally call for practice grids in the range of 20 yards wide by 25 yards long. Many coaches of young players unwittingly set up grids of this size for their teams even though such grids are too big for 6-and-under players.

We recommend you set up small grids of 15 yards by 20 yards for your young players. The smaller grid size will enable your players to successfully accomplish the various drills you'll play with them during your practice sessions. If your players are successful, they'll have fun during practice. If they have fun during practice, they'll keep playing—and learning—the game of soccer.

Here's what you'll need to do at your practice site before the start of each practice:

1. Arrive early enough to set up your practice grids before your players show up. Set up one grid, with "traffic lanes," to play Red Light/Green Light. (See diagram on page 67.) Each driving lane should be about 20 yards (or twenty paces) long and 3 yards (or three paces) wide. Assuming you have seven to twelve players on your team, set up a second rectangular grid. (See diagram on page 91.) This grid should be about 15 yards (or fifteen paces) wide by 20 yards (or twenty paces) long.
2. As your players arrive, greet them warmly and check their equipment to make sure they're ready to play.
3. Take on the responsibility yourself of assuring that all your players' cleats are double-tied. Double-tie those that aren't. It's a lot easier to do this before practice than when laces come untied in the middle of practice.

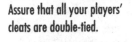

Assure that all your players' cleats are double-tied.

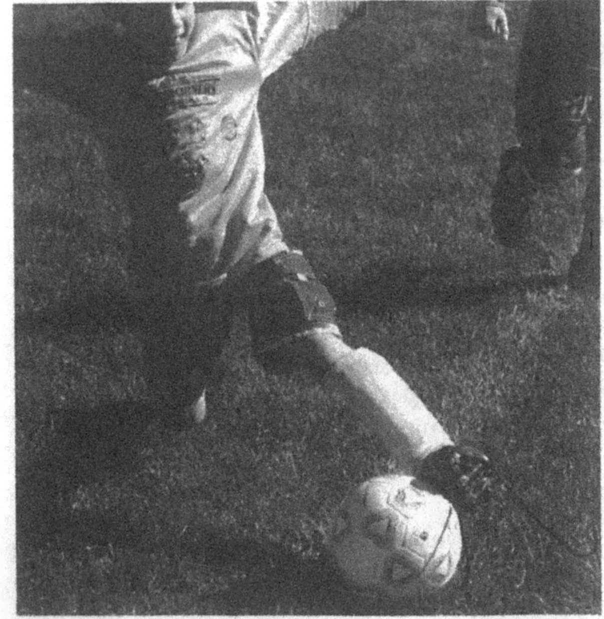

4. Be sure your players are wearing shin guards. Those who aren't should sit on the sidelines for any drills during which they may be kicked in the shins by other players.
5. Check your players' balls to be sure they're properly inflated (firm, but not rock-hard, to the touch). Inflate those that need it.
6. Hand out extra balls to those who need them.
7. As you get each player set, send him off to kick his ball around the field or into a goal if one is available at your practice site. After you've introduced juggling to your players (see Skill 6, pages 87–89), encourage them to juggle as a great way to get ready for practice.
8. For your first practice only: once you've readied and sent off all your players, gather

Participate!

It is vitally important for you and your parent helper to actively participate in the drills you run with your team. Your active participation in the drills will make those drills much more fun for your players, and as you know by now, *fun equals learning* for your players.

You'll be an active participant in Red Light/Green Light simply by shouting out traffic signals and moving among your players complimenting and helping them with their skills. You should be just as active a participant in the remainder of the drills you run each practice session. Take on the role of a crab in Crab Soccer. Be a swamp monster in the Alligator Pit or a space alien threatening to interfere with passes during Star Wars. Play Elmer Fudd and Freeze Tag right along with your players.

In all those cases, as an active participant in your team's drills, you'll be correctly positioned to spot and help your players with problems they may be having with their skills. In addition, you'll be in position to shield less aggressive players from more aggressive players. Plus, you'll be able to directly control the level of fun in each drill—injecting it with a bit more excitement by, for example, letting out a swamp-monster howl when things are slowing down, or subtly reining things in when your players get a bit too excited.

Best of all is what your active participation in your team's drills will do for *you.* You'll get your workout in for the day, and you'll have lots of fun each and every practice.

the parents before you. Distribute the first-practice handout you've prepared, as discussed in Chapter 4, Off the Field.

The handout will re-emphasize your coaching philosophy, which you've already expressed to the parents via e-mail. The handout also will list your players' equipment requirements. In addition, it will include the team roster, practice and game schedule, and assignments for halftime snacks, end-of-game treats, and the end-of-season celebration.

Take a moment to briefly describe to the parents the importance of your fun-based, touch-oriented coaching philosophy. Ask the parents to join you in always being positive and in playing down the idea of winning and losing games. Tell them you'll be happy to answer any questions after they've had a chance to read the handout, and thank them for giving you the opportunity to coach their children.

9. Assuming your team, like most, has between six and twelve players, recruit a parent helper from among your gathered parents (if you haven't recruited a parent beforehand). As detailed on pages 33–34, ask a parent to help for "just this one practice." Be sure to make your request when you have all the parents gathered before you to ensure peer pressure works in your favor.
10. Quickly describe to your parent helper the drill you'll need her to run with half the team in the rectangular grid while you'll be running the other half of the team through Red Light/Green Light in the driving-lanes grid.

During Practice

Now it's time to start your actual practice session.

Don't worry about running your players through a warm-up routine. Your players will have been running around and playing all day before practice. They'll be plenty warmed up already.

Call your players over and have them sit on their balls before you. Introduce yourself. Run through your players' names and offer a quick personal greeting to each. Let your players know, with plenty of enthusiasm, that you and they will be having lots of fun together this season.

Have half your players put on mesh bibs to divide your team into two squads. Or, if your players are wearing reversible jerseys, have half of them turn their shirts to one color on the outside, with the others wearing their shirts with the second color out. Randomly divide your team into different squads for every practice to ensure all your players get to practice with all their teammates. Be sure to divide your team into squads quickly, before your players have the chance to request a certain squad. Now send half the team, as demarcated by their shirt or bib color, off to play in the rectangular grid with your parent helper.

Run Red Light/Green Light as detailed in the driving-lanes grid while your parent helper runs the scheduled drill in his grid.

You'll be running all your drills, including Red Light/Green Light, in 10-minute increments. Note, however, that the 10 minutes include time for setting up the drill, switching from one drill to the next, and quick water breaks every 20 minutes. The actual amount of time your players will spend performing each drill will be 5 to 6 minutes—perfect for your 6-and-under players, whose attention spans roughly equate to 1 minute for every year of age.

If you have six or fewer players on your team or at practice, you won't need a parent helper.

If you have more than twelve players on your team, you'll need to set up two grids in addition to your driving-lanes grid, and you'll need to recruit two parent helpers. You'll then need to run your players through Red Light/Green Light in three segments rather than two.

Don't give in to the temptation to run Red Light/Green Light or any of the other drills with more than six players at a time. Teaching basic soccer skills to 6-and-under players is chaotic enough with up to six players. You'll only make things worse for your players and yourself if you overload the drills. If no one will agree to help you out, you'll be better off sitting players down among their waiting parents and working with no more than six at once than you will trying—and failing—to teach more than six players at a time all by yourself.

As you run each practice, remember that being creative is just as important a part of your coaching duties as it is a part of your team members' play on the field:

- Don't be afraid to *tweak the practice sessions* we've included here so that they work better for you and your players.
- *Go with the flow.* If a player spots a caterpillar in the grass, gather around with the rest of the team to study it and move it off the field to safety. If a talkative player needs to tell everyone about his toddler sister's incredibly runny nose, give him a moment to do so. If a really cool sports car passes by, stop and watch it with your players.
- Be a *storyteller*. As we noted in the preceding chapter, children age 6 and under *love* stories. When it's time for you to lead your players through each drill, don't tell them you're going to lead them through a drill. Don't even tell them you're going to play a game with them. Instead, intrigue them with an adventure.

  Feel free to use the story ideas provided with each drill, or make up your own.

After Practice

At the end of your first practice each season, lead your players through the process of selecting a new team name, as detailed on pages 43–44.

At the end of every practice, gather your players around you. Thank them for playing with you. Tell them what a great job they did, and let them know how much you're looking forward to the next game or practice. To finish up, have your players put their hands together with you and offer up a raucous team cheer.

4- and 5-Year-Old Practice Sessions

If your team consists primarily of 4- and 5-year-olds, practice sessions 1 through 6 on the following pages are for you.

Note that each practice session with these very young soccer players should last only 40 minutes—plenty of time given your players' tender ages.

Begin each practice by running half your team through Red Light/ Green Light while your parent helper runs the other half of your team through the drill specified for each practice session. Then switch squads and run the other half of your team through Red Light/Green Light while your parent helper repeats his drill with the team members you just finished working with.

When you're done introducing the skill designated for that particular practice by running both halves of your team through Red Light/Green Light, call a quick water break. While your players get drinks, remove the disc cones from the middle of your driving-lanes grid and those that form the outermost lane of the grid to create a second rectangular grid roughly 15 yards wide by 20 yards long. Quickly explain to your parent helper the next drill you need him to run in his grid, and then send half the team to

Red Light/Green Light

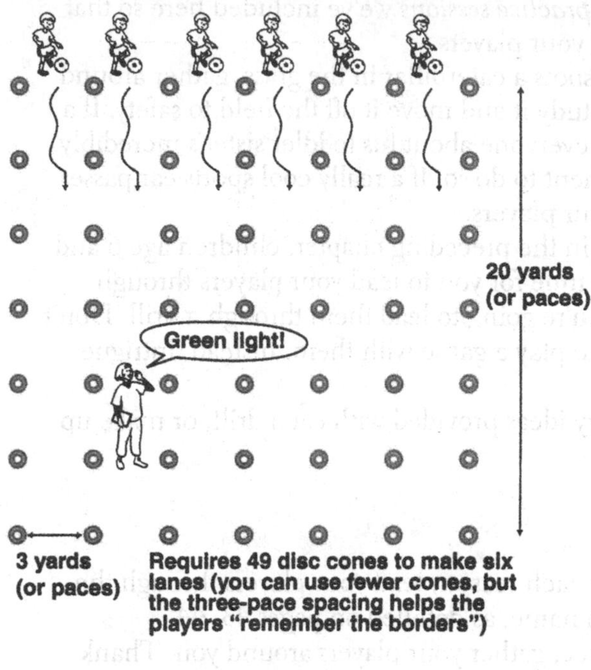
Green light!
20 yards
(or paces)
3 yards
(or paces)
Requires 49 disc cones to make six lanes (you can use fewer cones, but the three-pace spacing helps the players "remember the borders")

Regular Grid

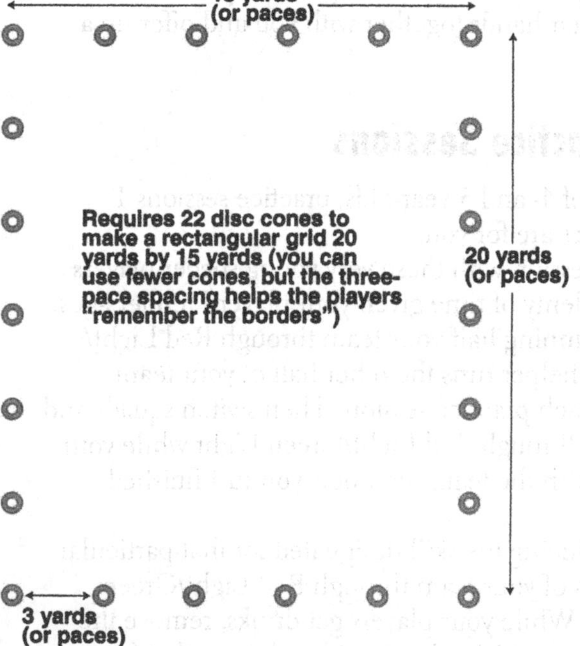
15 yards
(or paces)
Requires 22 disc cones to make a rectangular grid 20 yards by 15 yards (you can use fewer cones, but the three-pace spacing helps the players "remember the borders")
20 yards
(or paces)
3 yards
(or paces)

the parent-helper grid and half to your grid. Run the drills as specified on the following pages, then switch players with your parent helper and repeat the drills.

Remember to positively reinforce the basic ball-control skills while you lead your players through the drills scheduled for the second half of each practice. In addition, help your players with their shooting and passing skills, as detailed in the preceding chapter along with Drill 6: Trash Day, and Drill 8: Star Wars.

First Six Practice Sessions for 4- and 5-Year-Olds

These practice sessions are designed for teams of seven to twelve players. The total time of each session is 40 minutes.

1 Dribbling and Stopping the Ball

Before practice, read Skill 1: Dribbling with the Inside of the Foot and Stopping the Ball by Stepping on It (pages 70–74); Drill 1: Red Light/Green Light (page 67); Drill 2: Bulldozers and Builders (pages 92–94); Drill 3: Follow the Leader (pages 94–96); and Drill 4: Switch (pages 96–97).

Purpose of Red Light/Green Light: To use the proper part of the foot to dribble the ball; to stop the ball by stepping on it

Purpose of other drills: To dribble the ball under control

Before you begin:

1. Set up one driving-lanes grid for Red Light/Green Light
2. Set up one rectangular grid with cones inside for Bulldozers and Builders
3. Describe Bulldozers and Builders to parent helper, including suggested story line
4. Divide players into two squads

Coach's clock:

0 to 10 minutes

Driving-Lanes Grid: Red Light/Green Light (led by coach)

Use of traffic signals "Green light" for players to begin dribbling and "Red light" for players to stop dribbling and place one foot on top of the ball

Rectangular Grid: Bulldozers and Builders (led by parent helper)

10 to 20 minutes

Trade players with parent helper and repeat the drills

Brief water break

- Remove cones from inside rectangular grid
- Remove discs from driving-lanes grid to create second rectangular grid
- Describe Switch to parent helper, including suggested story line

20 to 30 minutes

Rectangular Grid 1: Follow the Leader (led by coach)
Rectangular Grid 2: Switch (led by parent helper)

30 to 40 minutes

Trade players with parent helper and repeat the drills

Dribbling with Speed

Before practice, read Skill 2: Dribbling with Speed (pages 74–77) and Drill 5: Alligator Pit (pages 97–98).

Purpose of Red Light/Green Light: To speed up with the ball and push the ball with the instep as a precursor to dribbling with the outside of the foot

Purpose of other drills: To speed up and slow down with the ball

Before you begin:

1. Set up one driving-lanes grid for Red Light/Green Light
2. Set up one rectangular practice grid
3. Divide players into two squads

Coach's clock:

0 to 10 minutes

Driving-Lanes Grid: Red Light/Green Light (led by coach)

Use of traffic signals "Green light" for players to begin dribbling, "Hit the highway" for players to accelerate with ball, and "Red light" for players to stop dribbling and place one foot on top of the ball

Rectangular Grid: Switch (led by parent helper)

10 to 20 minutes

Trade players with parent helper and repeat the drills

Brief water break

- Remove discs from driving-lanes grid to create second rectangular practice grid
- Place cones in rectangular grid for Alligator Pit
- Describe Follow the Leader to parent helper, including suggested story line

20 to 30 minutes

Rectangular Grid 1: Alligator Pit (led by coach)

Rectangular Grid 2: Follow the Leader (led by parent helper)

30 to 40 minutes

Trade players with parent helper and repeat the drills

3 Changing Direction with the Inside of the Foot, or "Cutting" the Ball

Before practice, read Skill 3: Changing Direction with the Inside of the Foot, or "Cutting" the Ball (pages 77–80); Skill 7: Kicking with the Instep (pages 99–101); and Drill 6: Trash Day (pages 98–99).

Purpose of Red Light/Green Light: To use the inside of the foot to cut the ball
Purpose of other drills: To change direction with the ball; in Trash Day, to kick with the instep, or shoot (see Skill 7: Kicking with the Instep)

Before you begin:

1. Set up one driving-lanes grid for Red Light/Green Light with cones in the middle of each driving lane
2. Set up one rectangular grid
3. Divide players into two squads

Coach's Clock:

0 to 10 minutes

Driving-Lanes Grid: Red Light/Green Light (led by coach)
Use of traffic signals "Green light" for players to begin dribbling, "Roundabout" for players to cut the balls around the cones placed in the middle of each driving lane, and "Red light" for players to stop dribbling and place one foot on top of the ball
Continued use of "Hit the highway" for players to accelerate with ball
Rectangular Grid: Follow the Leader (led by parent helper)

10 to 20 minutes

Trade players with parent helper and repeat the drills

Brief water break

- Remove discs and cones from driving-lanes grid to create second rectangular grid
- Place line of cones in grid for Trash Day
- Place cones in other rectangular grid for Alligator Pit
- Describe Alligator Pit to parent helper, including suggested story line

20 to 30 minutes

Rectangular Grid 1: Trash Day (led by coach)
Added skill: Kicking with the instep, or shooting
Rectangular Grid 2: Alligator Pit (led by parent helper)

30 to 40 minutes

Trade players with parent helper and repeat the drills

The Pull Turn

Before practice, read Skill 4: The Pull Turn (pages 80–83) and Drill 7: Elmer Fudd (pages 101–2).

Purpose of Red Light/Green Light: To use the bottom of the foot to perform a pull turn

Purpose of other drills: To change direction with a modified pull turn

Before you begin:

1. Set up one driving-lanes grid for Red Light/Green Light
2. Set up one rectangular practice grid
3. Divide players into two squads

Coach's Clock:

0 to 10 minutes

Driving-Lanes Grid: Red Light/Green Light (led by coach)

Use of traffic signals "Green light" for players to begin dribbling, "U-turn" for players to perform pull turns, and "Red light" for players to stop dribbling and place one foot on top of the ball

Continued use of "Hit the highway" for players to accelerate and "Roundabout" for players to cut the ball

Rectangular Grid: Follow the Leader (led by parent helper)

10 to 20 minutes

Trade players with parent helper and repeat the drills

Brief water break

- Remove discs from driving-lanes grid to create second rectangular grid
- Place line of cones in one grid for Trash Day
- Describe Trash Day to parent helper, including suggested story line and kicking with the instep

20 to 30 minutes

Rectangular Grid 1: Elmer Fudd (led by coach)

Opportunity for players to begin putting skills together, including dribbling under control, accelerating, stopping, cutting, kicking with instep, and pull turn

Rectangular Grid 2: Trash Day (led by parent helper)

Continued emphasis on kicking with the instep

30 to 40 minutes

Trade players with parent helper and repeat the drills

5 Receiving the Ball

Before practice, read Skill 5: Receiving the Ball (pages 84–86); Skill 8: Passing with the Inside of the Foot (pages 104–6); and Drill 8: Star Wars (pages 102–3).

Purpose of Red Light/Green Light: To trap the ball with the foot as a precursor to receiving passes in the air

Purpose of other drills: To receive and control a moving ball; in Star Wars, to pass with the inside of the foot (see Skill 8: Passing with the Inside of the Foot)

Before you begin:

1. Set up one driving-lanes grid for Red Light/Green Light
2. Set up one rectangular grid with cones placed inside for Alligator Pit
3. Divide players into two squads

Coach's clock:

0 to 10 minutes

Driving-Lanes Grid: Red Light/Green Light (led by coach)

Use of traffic signal "Out of the sky" for players to toss the ball into the air head high and then trap the ball against the ground with one foot

Continued use of "Green light" for players to begin dribbling, "Red light" for players to stop dribbling and place one foot on top of the ball, "Hit the highway" for players to accelerate, "Roundabout" for players to cut the ball, and "U-turn" for players to perform pull turns

Rectangular Grid: Alligator Pit (led by parent helper)

10 to 20 minutes

Trade players with parent helper and repeat the drills

Brief water break

- Remove discs from driving-lanes grid to create second rectangular grid
- Describe Elmer Fudd to parent helper, including suggested story line

20 to 30 minutes

Rectangular Grid 1: Star Wars (led by coach)

Played in grid already set up with cones inside

Rectangular Grid 2: Elmer Fudd (led by parent helper)

Continued opportunity for players to put skills together, including dribbling under control, accelerating, stopping, cutting, kicking with instep, and pull turn

30 to 40 minutes

Trade players with parent helper and repeat the drills

Juggling the Ball

Before practice, read Skill 6: Juggling the Ball (pages 87–89) and Drill 9: Crab Soccer (pages 106–7).

Purpose of Red Light/Green Light: To juggle the ball as a precursor to full ball control

Purpose of other drills: To control the ball; in Crab Soccer, to dribble under pressure

Before you begin:

1. Set up one driving-lanes grid for Red Light/Green Light
2. Set up one rectangular practice grid
3. Divide players into two squads

Coach's clock:

0 to 10 minutes

Driving-Lanes Grid: Red Light/Green Light (led by coach)

Use of traffic signal "Traffic jam" for players to attempt to juggle the ball one time off the instep

Continued use of "Green light" for players to begin dribbling, "Red light" for players to stop dribbling and place one foot on top of the ball, "Hit the highway" for players to accelerate, "Roundabout" for players to cut the ball, "U-turn" for players to perform pull turns, and "Out of the sky" for trapping

Rectangular Grid: Elmer Fudd (led by parent helper)

10 to 20 minutes

Trade players with parent helper and repeat the drills

Brief water break

- Remove discs from driving-lanes grid to create second rectangular grid
- Place cones in one rectangular grid for Star Wars drill
- Describe Star Wars to parent helper, including suggested story line and passing with the inside of the foot

20 to 30 minutes

Rectangular Grid 1: Crab Soccer (led by coach)

Opportunity for players to experience dribbling under pressure

Note: *If players don't respond well to dribbling under pressure while playing Crab Soccer, don't push it—wait a couple of weeks, or even until next season*

Rectangular Grid 2: Star Wars (led by parent helper)

30 to 40 minutes

Trade players with parent helper and repeat the drills

Specifics for 5- and 6-Year-Old Practice Sessions

If your team consists primarily of 5- and 6-year-old soccer players rather than 4- and 5-year-olds, the following practice sessions are for you. These sessions involve slightly more advanced drills than those for 4- and 5-year olds. In addition, these sessions involve drills that will introduce 5- and 6-year-old players to the ideas of competition and competitiveness in ways that you, as coach, control.

Note that each of your practice sessions with your slightly older soccer players will last 60 minutes rather than the 40 minutes adequate for very young players.

Begin each practice by running half your team through Red Light/ Green Light while your parent helper runs the other half of the team through the drill specified for each practice session. Then switch squads and run the other half of your team through Red Light/Green Light while your parent helper repeats her drill with the team members you just finished working with.

When you're done introducing the skill designated for that particular practice by running both halves of your team through Red Light/Green Light, call a quick water break. While your players get drinks, remove the disc cones from the middle of your driving-lanes grid and those that form the outer lane of the grid to create a second rectangular grid roughly 15 yards wide by 20 yards long. Quickly explain to your parent helper the next drill you need her to run in her grid and then send half the team to the parent helper's grid and half to your grid. Run the drills as specified on the following pages and then switch players with your parent helper and repeat the drills.

Take another water break at the 40-minute mark and then run your players through two more drills, in 10-minute increments, with your parent helper.

Remember to continue positively reinforcing the basic ball-control skills while you lead the fun drills with your players for the final two-thirds of each practice. In addition, help your players with shooting, passing, receiving the ball on the ground, and shielding, as detailed in the preceding chapter along with Drill 6: Trash Day, Drill 8: Star Wars, Drill 11: Steal the Bacon, and Drill 12: Freeze Tag.

First Six Practice Sessions for 5- and 6-Year-Olds

These practice sessions are designed for teams of seven to twelve players. The total time of each session is 60 minutes.

1 Dribbling and Stopping the Ball

Before practice, read Skill 1: Dribbling with the Inside of the Foot and Stopping the Ball by Stepping on It (pages 70–74); Skill 7: Kicking with the Instep (pages 99–101); Drill 1: Red Light/Green Light (page 67); Drill 2: Bulldozers and Builders (pages 92–94); Drill 5: Alligator Pit (pages 97–98); Drill 6: Trash Day (pages 98–99); Drill 7: Elmer Fudd (pages 101–2); and Drill 9: Crab Soccer (pages 106–7).

Purpose of Red Light/Green Light: To use the proper part of the foot to dribble the ball; to stop the ball by stepping on it

Purpose of other drills: To dribble the ball under control; in Trash Day, to kick with the instep, or shoot (see Skill 7: Kicking with the Instep); in Crab Soccer, to dribble under pressure

Before you begin:

1. Set up one driving-lanes grid for Red Light/Green Light
2. Set up one rectangular grid with cones inside for Bulldozers and Builders
3. Describe Bulldozers and Builders to parent helper, including suggested story line
4. Divide players into two squads

Coach's clock:

0 to 10 minutes

Driving-Lanes Grid: Red Light/Green Light (led by coach)

Use of traffic signals "Green light" for players to begin dribbling and "Red light" for players to stop dribbling and place one foot on top of the ball

Rectangular Grid: Bulldozers and Builders (led by parent helper)

10 to 20 minutes

Trade players with parent helper and repeat the drills

Brief water break

- Remove discs from driving-lanes grid to create second rectangular grid
- Place line of cones inside grid for Trash Day
- Use grid already set up with cones inside for Alligator Pit
- Describe Alligator Pit to parent helper, including suggested story line

20 to 30 minutes
Rectangular Grid 1: Trash Day (led by coach)
Added skill: Kicking with the instep, or shooting
Rectangular Grid 2: Alligator Pit (led by parent helper)

30 to 40 minutes
Trade players with parent helper and repeat the drills

Brief water break
- Remove cones from both grids
- Describe Elmer Fudd to parent helper, including suggested story line

40 to 50 minutes
Rectangular Grid 1: Crab Soccer (led by coach)
Opportunity for players to experience dribbling under pressure
Rectangular Grid 2: Elmer Fudd (led by parent helper)

50 to 60 minutes
Trade players with parent helper and repeat the drills

2 Dribbling with Speed

Before practice, read Skill 2: Dribbling with Speed (pages 74–77) and Drill 10: Sharks and Minnows (pages 107–9).

Purpose of Red Light/Green Light: To speed up with the ball and push the ball with the instep as a precursor to dribbling with the outside of the foot

Purpose of other drills: To speed up and slow down with the ball

Before you begin:

1. Set up one driving-lanes grid for Red Light/Green Light
2. Set up one rectangular grid with cones inside for Alligator Pit
3. Divide players into two squads

Coach's clock:

0 to 10 minutes

Driving-Lanes Grid: Red Light/Green Light (led by coach)

Use of traffic signals "Green light" for players to begin dribbling, "Hit the highway" for players to accelerate with ball, and "Red light" for players to stop dribbling and place one foot on top of the ball

Rectangular Grid: Alligator Pit (led by parent helper)

10 to 20 minutes

Trade players with parent helper and repeat the drills

Brief water break

- Remove discs from driving-lanes grid to create second rectangular grid
- Place line of cones in grid for Trash Day
- Remove cones from inside grid used for Alligator Pit

20 to 30 minutes

Rectangular Grid 1: Trash Day (led by coach)

Rectangular Grid 2: Elmer Fudd (led by parent helper)

30 to 40 minutes

Trade players with parent helper and repeat the drills

Brief water break

- Remove cones from grid used for Trash Day
- Describe Crab Soccer drill to parent helper, including suggested story line

40 to 50 minutes

Rectangular Grid 1: Sharks and Minnows (led by coach)

As with Crab Soccer, further opportunity for players to experience dribbling under pressure

Rectangular Grid 2: Crab Soccer (led by parent helper)

50 to 60 minutes

Trade players with parent helper and repeat the drills

3 Changing Direction with the Inside of the Foot, or "Cutting" the Ball

Before practice, read Skill 3: Changing Direction with the Inside of the Foot, or "Cutting" the Ball (pages 77–80); Skill 8: Passing with the Inside of the Foot (pages 104–6); and Drill 8: Star Wars (pages 102–3).

Purpose of Red Light/Green Light: To use the inside of the foot to cut the ball

Purpose of other drills: To change direction with the ball; in Star Wars, to pass with the inside of the foot (see Skill 8: Passing with the Inside of the Foot)

Before you begin:

1. Set up one driving-lanes grid for Red Light/Green Light with cones in the middle of each driving lane
2. Set up one rectangular grid with cones arranged inside for Alligator Pit
3. Divide players into two squads

Coach's clock:

0 to 10 minutes

Driving-Lanes Grid: Red Light/Green Light (led by coach)

Use of traffic signals "Green light" for players to begin dribbling, "Roundabout" for players to cut the ball around the cones placed in the middle of each driving lane, and "Red light" for players to stop dribbling and place one foot on top of the ball

Continued use of "Hit the highway" for players to accelerate

Rectangular Grid: Alligator Pit (led by parent helper)

10 to 20 minutes

Trade players with parent helper and repeat the drills

Brief water break

- Remove discs and cones from driving-lanes grid to create second rectangular grid
- Remove cones from grid used for Alligator Pit

20 to 30 minutes

Rectangular Grid 1: Elmer Fudd (led by coach)

Rectangular Grid 2: Crab Soccer (led by parent helper)

30 to 40 minutes
Trade players with parent helper and repeat the drills

Brief water break
- Describe Sharks and Minnows to parent helper
- Place cones in grid for Star Wars

40 to 50 minutes
Rectangular Grid 1: Star Wars (led by coach)
Rectangular Grid 2: Sharks and Minnows (led by parent helper)

50 to 60 minutes
Trade players with parent helper and repeat the drills

The Pull Turn

Before practice, read Skill 4: The Pull Turn (pages 80–83); Skill 9: Receiving the Ball on the Ground (page 112); and Drill 11: Steal the Bacon (pages 109–11).

Purpose of Red Light/Green Light: To use the bottom of the foot to perform a pull turn

Purpose of other drills: To change direction with a modified pull turn; in Steal the Bacon, to receive a pass on the ground, and experience game-like competition

Before you begin:

1. Set up one driving-lanes grid for Red Light/Green Light
2. Set up one rectangular grid with cones inside for Alligator Pit
3. Divide players into two squads

Coach's clock:

0 to 10 minutes

Driving-Lanes Grid: Red Light/Green Light (led by coach)

Use of traffic signals "Green light" for players to begin dribbling, "U-turn" for players to perform pull turns, and "Red light" for players to stop dribbling and place one foot on top of the ball

Continued use of "Hit the highway" for players to accelerate and "Roundabout" for players to cut the ball

Rectangular Grid: Alligator Pit (led by parent helper)

10 to 20 minutes

Trade players with parent helper and repeat the drills

Brief water break

- Remove discs from driving-lanes grid to create second rectangular grid
- Remove cones from grid used for Alligator Pit

20 to 30 minutes

Rectangular Grid 1: Elmer Fudd (led by coach)

Rectangular Grid 2: Sharks and Minnows (led by parent helper)

30 to 40 minutes

Trade players with parent helper and repeat the drills

Brief water break

- Place cones as goals at ends of grid for Steal the Bacon
- Place cones in grid for Star Wars
- Describe Star Wars to parent helper, including story line and passing with the inside of the foot

40 to 50 minutes

Rectangular Grid 1: Steal the Bacon (led by coach)
Opportunity for players to experience game-like competition under control of coach
Rectangular Grid 2: Star Wars (led by parent helper)

50 to 60 minutes

Trade players with parent helper and repeat the drills

5 Receiving the Ball

Before practice, read Skill 5: Receiving the Ball (pages 84–86); Skill 10: Shielding the Ball (pages 115–16); and Drill 12: Freeze Tag (pages 113–15).

Purpose of Red Light/Green Light: To trap the ball with the foot as a precursor to receiving passes in the air

Purpose of other drills: To receive and control a moving ball; in Freeze Tag, to shield the ball (see Skill 10: Shielding the Ball)

Before you begin:

1. Set up one driving-lanes grid for Red Light/Green Light
2. Set up one rectangular grid with cones inside for Alligator Pit
3. Divide players into two squads

Coach's clock:

0 to 10 minutes

Driving-Lanes Grid: Red Light/Green Light (led by coach)

Use of traffic signal "Out of the sky" for players to toss the ball into the air head high and then trap the ball against the ground with one foot

Continued use of "Green light" for players to begin dribbling, "Red light" for players to stop dribbling and place a foot on top of the ball, "Hit the highway" for players to accelerate, "Roundabout" for players to cut the ball, and "U-turn" for players to perform pull turns

Rectangular Grid: Alligator Pit (led by parent helper)

10 to 20 minutes

Trade players with parent helper and repeat the drills

Brief water break

Remove discs from driving-lanes grid to create second rectangular grid

20 to 30 minutes

Rectangular Grid 1: Sharks and Minnows (led by coach)

Rectangular Grid 2: Star Wars (led by parent helper)

30 to 40 minutes

Trade players with parent helper and repeat the drills

Brief water break

- Remove cones from grid used for Star Wars
- Place cones as goals at ends of grid for Steal the Bacon
- Describe Steal the Bacon to parent helper, including receiving the ball

40 to 50 minutes

Rectangular Grid 1: Freeze Tag (led by coach)
Rectangular Grid 2: Steal the Bacon (led by parent helper)

50 to 60 minutes

Trade players with parent helper and repeat the drills

6 Juggling the Ball

Before practice, read Skill 6: Juggling the Ball (pages 87–89).

Purpose of Red Light/Green Light: To juggle the ball as a precursor to full ball control

Purpose of other drills: To control the ball

Before you begin:

1. Set up one driving-lanes grid for Red Light/Green Light
2. Set up one rectangular grid with cones inside for Alligator Pit
3. Divide players into two squads

Coach's clock:

0 to 10 minutes

Driving-Lanes Grid: Red Light/Green Light (led by coach)

Use of traffic signal "Traffic jam" for players to attempt to juggle the ball one time off the instep

Continued use of "Green light" for players to begin dribbling, "Red light" for players to stop dribbling and place one foot on top of the ball, "Hit the highway" for players to accelerate, "Roundabout" for players to cut the ball, "U-turn" for players to perform pull turns, and "Out of the sky" for trapping

Rectangular Grid: Alligator Pit (led by parent helper)

10 to 20 minutes

Trade players with parent helper and repeat the drills

Brief water break

- Remove discs from driving-lanes grid to create second rectangular grid
- Remove cones from grid used for Alligator Pit
- Describe Freeze Tag to parent helper, including suggested story line and shielding the ball

20 to 30 minutes

Rectangular Grid 1: Elmer Fudd (led by coach)

Rectangular Grid 2: Freeze Tag (led by parent helper)

30 to 40 minutes

Trade players with parent helper and repeat the drills

Brief water break
Place cones as goals at ends of grid for Steal the Bacon

40 to 50 minutes
Rectangular Grid 1: Sharks and Minnows (led by coach)
Rectangular Grid 2: Steal the Bacon (led by parent helper)

50 to 60 minutes
Trade players with parent helper and repeat the drills

After Your First Six Practices

By the time you've led your team through the first six practices detailed in this chapter, you'll have enough experience to decide what drills to do with your team during subsequent practices. We recommend you continue to begin your practices with Red Light/Green Light to better reinforce the basic ball-control skills you'll introduce to your players during the first six practices. As far as selecting drills to round out the remaining practices in your season, possibilities include:

1. Starting over and running straight through the first six practices a second time. (Doing so is, in fact, a fine idea.)
2. Planning and running practice sessions that emphasize those drills your players enjoy most.
3. Planning and running practice sessions that emphasize the skills your players are having the most difficulty mastering.
4. For a team of 4- and 5-year-olds, experimenting with more advanced drills if you believe your team is ready for them. That would mean selecting from among Drill 10: Sharks and Minnows, Drill 11: Steal the Bacon, and Drill 12: Freeze Tag—the three slightly competitive drills suggested for 5- and 6-year-olds.

If you choose to add a more competitive drill to a practice session, be sure to add it at the end of practice when your players will be most relaxed and ready for it.

Parent/Player Scrimmages

Q. I've heard of coaches who hold a parent-versus-player scrimmage in place of their last practice each season. That sounds like lots of fun—and a way for parents to see, on the field, how much their kids' skills have improved over the course of the season. Why don't you recommend I hold a parent/player scrimmage instead of the last practice of the season?

A. You're right in noting that many coaches love the idea of parents scrimmaging with their children at the end of each season. We've seen many scrimmages between young players and their parents over the years.

We recommend you don't hold such a scrimmage between your young players and their parents for the same reason you never see parents scrimmaging with their 14-year-old soccer-playing children. In both cases, the games are unfair and, as a result, no fun for the weaker team.

In the case of teenagers versus parents, the teenagers are far better players than their parents and so must take it easy on the old folks to keep the game "close." No one likes being pandered to, least of all parents by their children. As a result, we've never seen a succesful scrimmage between a team of 14-year-olds and their outgunned parents. In the same way, it's rude for parents to pander to their young, soccer-playing children.

Any group of parents can easily defeat any team of 6-and-under players in a scrimmage, no matter how well coached the 6-and-under team may be. Even parents who have never played soccer understand how to pass the ball. They tend to have a great time during parent/kid scrimmages passing quickly to one another while their children chase along behind the ball in a big herd.

The problem with such a scenario is that, in the midst of having all that fun, the parents tend to forget one important fact: their kids are smart.

Six-and-under players may not be mature enough to assign themselves one player to each parent on defense, or to pass the ball back and forth to one another as they move the ball up the field on offense. But they're smart enough to know when they're being made fun of by their parents—even if their parents are making fun of them unknowingly. They know when their parents are taking it easy on them to keep the game "close" and to ensure that the children "win" the game. Such a situation damages children's self-esteem. There should be no place for it on your soccer field.

It's worth noting as well that parents tend to get overly aggressive when they take the field with their children. (We know because we've been guilty of over-aggressiveness on the field with youngsters ourselves.) As a result, one or two players invariably get run down and injured—physically, mentally, or both—by adults in scrimmages between parents and young players.

Finally, because most parents haven't played much soccer, they can't control their kicks very well. If you decide to hold a parent/kid scrimmage, there is the very real possibility that a parent will kick the ball too hard into the face or stomach of one of your young players, resulting in a bloody nose or, worse, a child who no longer enjoys the game of soccer.

Rather than facing their parents in an end-of-season scrimmage, your players will be far better off if you simply take a moment before the last game to point out to their parents how much every member of the team has improved over the course of the season, and how incredibly proud you are of all of them. (If possible, do so within earshot of your players.)

The End of the Season

Congratulations! You've completed your season as a 6-and-under soccer coach.

Now where do you go from here?

If your team members will be 6 or under for another season or more, continue to work from the practice sessions in this book—and enjoy watching your players' skills improve as your players mature.

When your players move beyond age 6, it'll be time for you to move beyond this book. We highly recommend you move on to Bobby Clark's *Coaching Youth Soccer: The Baffled Parent's Guide*. Clark promotes the same fun-based coaching philosophy we promote in this book, but with practice sessions and competitive drills appropriate for older players. For more than a hundred additional creative games for older players, check out *Great Soccer Drills: The Baffled Parent's Guide*, by Tom Fleck and Ron Quinn.

Skills Troubleshooting Chart

Skill 1: Dribbling with the Inside of the Foot and Stopping the Ball by Stepping on It (see pages 70–74)

Problem	Solution
Kicking the ball with the toes	Get down on your knees and press the inside of the player's foot against the ball to show exactly how to strike the ball – with inside of the foot near the toes
Dribbling too fast	Demonstrate correct pace by jogging alongside players without the ball
Dribbling too slowly	Encourage players to keep the ball moving
Striking the ball too hard	Show players the maximum distance the ball should be ahead of them (1–2 yards)
Tripping over the ball	Explain to players that they should reach ahead slightly with the foot each time they strike the ball

Skill 2: Dribbling with Speed (see pages 74–77)

Problem	Solution
Kicking the ball with the toes	Get down on your knees and press the inside of the player's foot against the ball to show exactly how to strike the ball – with the laces
Allowing the ball to fall back between the legs	Explain that when they speed up, players should keep the ball far enough out in front of them that they must take a big step forward each time they strike it

Skill 3: Changing Direction with the Inside of the Foot, or "Cutting" the Ball (see pages 77–80)

Problem	Solution
Running all the way around the ball	Explain that players should herd the ball around their cones quickly, using little kicks with the outside foot
Failing to pivot the inside foot	Demonstrate the way players must get the inside leg out of the way and pivot the inside foot so the outside foot may swing across to strike the ball
Touching the ball too many times	Encourage players to use fewer touches each turn

Skill 4: The Pull Turn (see pages 80–83)

Problem	Solution
Turning away from the ball during the pull turn	Encourage players to watch the ball all the way through the turn
Using the heel to stop the ball and initiate the pull turn	Demonstrate stepping on the ball to initiate the turn
Using the toes to stop the ball and initiate the pull turn	Demonstrate stepping on the ball to initiate the turn

Skill 5: Receiving the Ball (see pages 84–86)

Problem	Solution
Stopping after trapping the ball	Tell players to never let the ball stop moving
Not raising the foot high enough, or stepping on the ball too hard	Explain that players should think not of stepping on the *ground,* but of lifting the foot high enough to step lightly down on the *ball*
Ongoing difficulties with the skill	Suggest that players drop the ball from the waist rather than tossing the ball in the air head high

Skill 6: Juggling the Ball (see pages 87–89)

Problem	Solution
Extreme frustration	Offer lots of encouragement
Swinging the leg fully extended at the ball	Explain that players should swing only the lower leg at the ball, popping the ball with the instep to propel the ball straight up into the air

Skill 7: Kicking with the Instep, or Shooting (see pages 99–101)

Problem	Solution
Kicking with the toes	Encourage kicking with the laces and pointing the toes
Kicking with a straight leg	Explain that in the backswing, the heel should nearly kick players in the bottom
Missing the ball completely	Make sure players watch the ball all the way through the kick
No power	Have players land on the kicking foot, effectively taking a step forward

Skill 8: Passing with the Inside of the Foot (see pages 104–6)

Problem	Solution
Not kicking with the inside of the foot	The best way to teach players the correct foot position for passing with the inside of the foot is to walk around like a duck and have players mimic you. Swing both your feet out wide, raise your toes, and rock back on your heels. Now waddle around the field with your players as they do the same thing. Remember—and this is critical—quacking and wing flapping are mandatory
Kicking with a straight leg	Remind players to bend the knee
Missing the ball completely	Encourage players to watch the ball all the way through the kick
No power	Explain to players that the kicking foot should rise high enough off the ground after the kick for the sole to be visible to an onlooker standing in front of the passing player

Skill 9: Receiving the Ball on the Ground (see page 112)

Problem	Solution
Ball rolling past players	Encourage players to move into the path of the ball so the ball at least hits them
Lifting the foot too high	Remind players to watch the ball roll all the way in to the foot
Kicking the ball instead of receiving it	Encourage players to stop the ball first, then start dribbling

Skill 10: Shielding the Ball (see pages 115–16)

Problem	Solution
Defenders kicking between legs and knocking ball away	Demonstrate to players how they should be sideways to defenders and should not turn their backs on defenders

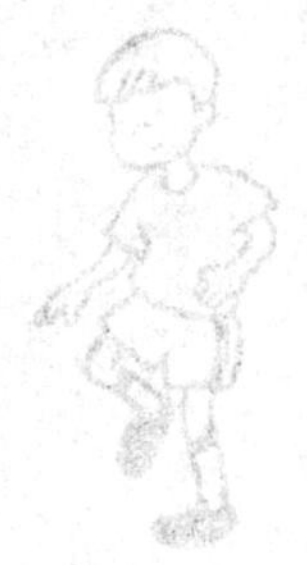

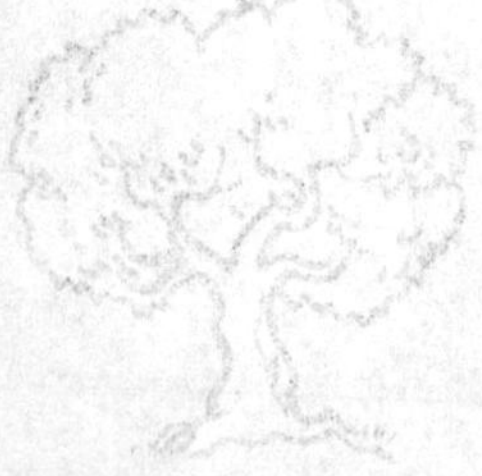

Resources

Websites

U.S. Youth Soccer Association at www.usyouthsoccer.org
Largest youth soccer association in the country. More rules, laws, and news about youth soccer than you could ever hope to read. U.S. Youth Soccer actively promotes small-sided soccer for young soccer players (see pages 16–19 in this book). For more on small-sided soccer on the association's website, click on the Coaches link, then click on "Small-Sided Games Resource Center" under Related Topics, and then on the "Why Small-Sided Games?" article.

American Youth Soccer Organization at www.soccer.org
Second-largest youth soccer association in the country. American Youth Soccer extended its programs to players as young as 4 — down from age 5 — in 2005. Like U.S. Youth Soccer, American Youth Soccer promotes small-sided soccer for young players, though American Youth Soccer uses the term "short-sided soccer." See the organization's guidelines for young players by clicking on "programs," then "short-sided games."

National Alliance for Youth Sports at www.nays.org
Promotes good sportsmanship in youth sports. The alliance is the umbrella organization for the Parents Association for Youth Sports and the National Youth Sports Coaches Association. The parents association educates parents, advocates good behavior by parents, and challenges its parent members to adhere to a code of ethics. The coaches association is the most widely used volunteer coach training program in the nation, having trained more than 1.8 million coaches since its inception in 1981.

Books

Coaching Youth Soccer: The Baffled Parent's Guide, by Bobby Clark
The best-selling soccer coaching book in the country, written by one of the world's soccer greats, Notre Dame coach Bobby Clark. This witty, highly readable book will help prepare you for the demands you'll eventually face as a coach of players over age 6. The book contains plenty of tips, hints, and drills that will help you as a coach of 6-and-under players as well.

Great Soccer Drills: The Baffled Parent's Guide, by Tom Fleck and Ron Quinn
Are the 12 drills presented in *Coaching 6-and-Under Soccer* simply not enough for you? Fleck and Quinn offer 125 dynamic games in their book, which is filled with pictures and diagrams that make trying out new games with your players easy.

Just Let the Kids Play: How to Stop Other Adults from Ruining Your Child's Fun and Success in Youth Sports, by youth-sports expert Bob Bigelow and journalists Tom Moroney and Linda Hall

The best of several books out on the subject of over-the-top competitiveness in American youth sports today and the problems associated with it. A must-read for any coaches of young players who still believe, despite having read *Coaching 6-and-Under Soccer*, that it's never too early to instill hypercompetitiveness in young athletes.

It's Not About the Bra: Play Hard, Play Fair, and Put the Fun Back into Competitive Sports, by Brandi Chastain with Gloria Averbuch
Chastain, a member of the Olympic and World Cup champion U.S. Women's National Soccer Team, offers numerous anecdotes from her own storied career and those of her coaches and teammates as she tackles the thorny issues of sportsmanship, gamesmanship, and parental involvement gone too far in American youth sports today. She offers a blueprint for coaches on how to teach their players to play fair, win and lose with grace, and, above all, have a good time while practicing and competing.

The Vision of a Champion: Advice and Inspiration from the World's Most Successful Women's Soccer Coach, by Anson Dorrance and Gloria Averbuch
Dorrance is the winningest women's soccer coach of all time, with eighteen national championships as head coach of the University of North Carolina Women's Soccer Team. In this book, he teams with health and fitness writer Averbuch to offer his formula for success both on and off the soccer field through a unique blend of technical and inspirational advice.

Index

Numbers in **bold** refer to pages with illustrations

Acknowledgments

We would like to express our sincere thanks to the many fellow young-player soccer coaches we've worked and coached with over the years. Their dedication to young soccer players, their willingness to try the different drills in this book (and many that didn't make the cut), their willingness to read the manuscript in its formative stages—all have made this book far better than it otherwise would have been.

About the Authors

David Williams is a lifelong soccer player and coach, and a former computer-industry executive turned at-home dad. He lives in Durango, Colorado, with his wife, son, and daughter. Williams's specific interest in coaching young players has led to his heading up the 4- and 5-year-old division of the series of summer soccer camps sponsored by the Fort Lewis College soccer team in Durango.

Scott Graham is a full-time at-home dad and a part-time writer. He lives in Durango, Colorado, with his wife and two sons. Graham is the author of *Extreme Kids: How to Connect with Your Children Through Today's Extreme—and Not so Extreme—Outdoor Sports* (Wilderness Press) and *Handle with Care: A Guide to Responsible Travel in Developing Countries* (Noble Press), among others.